HIMALAYAS

Photographs and Text by **YOSHIKAZU SHIRAKAWA**

HIMA

Preface by

ARNOLD TOYNBEE

Introduction by

SIR EDMUND HILLARY

Essay, ''The Great Himalayas,'' by

KYUYA FUKADA

HARRY N. ABRAMS, INC., PUBLISHERS, NEW YORK

Library of Congress Cataloging in Publication Data
Shirakawa, Yoshikazu, 1935-
  HIMALAYAS.
  Original Japanese ed. published under title:
Himaraya.
  1. Himalaya Mountains—Description and travel.
I. Title.
DS485.H6S42713   1977   954   76-47575
ISBN 0-8109-1051-9

ⓒ 1976 by Mondadori - Shogakukan
Photograph copyright ⓒ 1976 by Yoshikazu Shirakawa
Text copyright ⓒ 1976 by Mondadori - Shogakukan

Library of Congress Catalog Card Number: 76-47575
Original English-language edition published in the United States by Harry N. Abrams, Inc.
Original Japanese edition published by Shogakukan Publishing Co. Ltd., Tokyo
This concise edition published in 1977 by Harry N. Abrams, Inc., New York

Printed in Italy by Officine Grafiche Arnoldo Mondadori - Verona

CONTENTS

I have gazed, with awe, at some of the high peaks of the Himalayas on a journey by air from Rawalpindi to Gilgit. From an aeroplane the traveller's glimpses of the World are brief. Sometimes, indeed, he sees nothing, from taking-off to landing, except the upper surface of a continuous blanket of cloud. On this journey I was fortunate. I did see the mighty mountains, and my vision of them has made an ineffaceable impression on my mind. I was overwhelmed by their beauty, and their majesty, and at the same time I realised that here Nature was revealing to me something that is beyond herself. The splendour that shines through Nature is imparted to her from a source which is beyond Nature and which is the ultimate reality. If there were not this invisible spiritual presence in and beyond the visible universe, there would be no Himalayas and no mankind either; for mankind is part of Nature, and, like non-human Nature, we owe our existence to the reality that is the mysterious common source of non-human Nature and ourselves.

As I flew over the Himalayas, I felt the cold rise from the peaks far down below me and shoot up through the floor of the plane to chill my feet and legs. For a moment, Nature seemed more powerful than even modern Man. Surely the Himalayas are inviolable. Yet this man-made man-piloted plane was soaring over them, and one peak after another had already been scaled to the summit. So are the Himalayas really secure against Man's assaults, now that Man is armed with a scientific technology? May it not now be within Man's power to desecrate the Himalayas if he finds this economically profitable and militarily advantageous?

We have not yet succeeded in defiling and defacing the Himalayas. For the time being, they remain inviolate. But we have already polluted and marred the more easily accessible parts of the land and water surface of our planet. One of the most beautiful countries on Earth is Japan. Yet the Japanese people themselves have been spoiling their homeland. They have been obliterating the plains under a hideous man-made crust of streets and apartment-houses and factories. They have been gashing the shapely mountains to cut speedways through them. They have been poisoning their air with fumes and their waters with refuse. And, over plain and mountain alike, they have been spreading a pall of smog which veils the country and starves it of sunlight.

This brutal treatment of non-human Nature has now been carried to extreme lengths in Japan, but it was started at the opposite end of the Old World, in Britain. This was the birthplace of the Industrial Revolution that has spread all round the globe within the last two hundred years. Within these two centuries, Man has enormously increased his power by harnessing the inanimate forces of Nature on an unprecedented scale. He has only just begun to realise that, in enslaving Nature, he is threatening to liquidate himself. Man is a part of Nature, and he will not be able to survive if he destroys the natural environment in which his pre-human ancestors became human in the act of awaking to consciousness.

From the beginning of this human chapter of his history, Man has been bent on mastering Nature, and he has now succeeded in mastering the whole of terrestrial Nature except himself. This is an ironical achievement and an ironical failure. Self-mastery is, for Man, the key to happiness, to welfare, and to survival. Yet human nature is still recalcitrant to Man's command, and this unregenerate human nature is a threat to Man's existence, now that Man has armed himself with inanimate Nature's titanic forces.

Man has now fallen into conflict with human and non-human Nature alike. This is why, today, his enhanced power and wealth are causing him increasing anxiety and unhappiness. But this present-day disharmony dates only from the invention of mechanised industry. Pre-industrial Man, the hunter and the cultivator, managed to make Nature minister to his needs without going to War with her. Upper Palaeolithic Man's cave-paintings show that he was fascinated by the beauty and prowess of the animals on whom he preyed. Neolithic Man made the face of the Earth more beautiful by transmuting the wilderness into rice-paddies and corn-fields. Till the Industrial Revolution in England, only two hundred years ago, Man still lived at peace with Nature. He still felt the awe of Nature that he had inherited from ancestors who had been at Nature's mercy. Cannot we regain this lost ancient concord between Man and his environment?

Since Man became conscious, he has been aware that he himself is not the spiritually highest presence in the universe, and he has been seeking to communicate with this higher form of reality in order to put himself into harmony with it. His earliest avenue of approach to it was through his natural environment. He worshipped the ultimate reality through the manifestations of it in mountains, such as the beautiful and majestic Himalayas, and in forests, springs, rivers, and the ocean.

At the Western end of the Old World and in the Americas this earliest form of religion has been killed by monotheism in the forms of Judaism, Christianity, and Islam. But in India and Eastern Asia the worship of ultimate reality through the medium of Nature still survives. I have twice visited Ise, the holiest seat of Shinto. The lovely valley in which Ise lies is a meeting-place between virgin tree-clad mountains and a plain that Man has transformed, without defacing it, by turning it into an exquisite pattern of rice-paddies. At Ise, standing at the entrance to the shrine, I have felt what I felt when I was flying over the Himalayas. Through the beauty and the majesty of Nature, I found myself communicating with Nature's and Man's common source.

The Japanese people have not bulldozed Ise and have not repudiated Shinto. They have obliterated the natural beauty of the shores of the Shimonoseki Straits, which I myself saw, still unspoiled, as recently as 1929. They have almost vulgarised Nara. But Ise remains sacrosanct and intact, and Ise, like the Himalayas, has a message to give to Man in an age when he is being menaced by the backfire of his latest technological achievements. The message is one of hope. It is still possible for Man to regain his original concord with Nature, and this will bring him salvation from his present Man-made plight.

Arnold Toynbee

8

Men the world over have looked to the mountains for inspiration and refreshment. For twenty years I have walked and climbed in the Himalayas and each time has been just as exciting and stimulating as my first visit.

There is so much to see and much to do. The lack of roads and modern methods of transport force the adventurous visitor to travel on foot over the steep hill paths—but surely this is an advantage even for the city dweller who aims to cram the maximum of experience into the shortest possible space of time.

In Nepal the tempo is slower. As you walk the body gets strong; the mind has time to dwell on the beauties of nature and gain refreshment; you meet the local people, the Sherpas; and enjoy their cheerful friendliness and admire their toughness and strength; you breathe good clean air again. . . .

Above the villages the streams run clear and sparkling and their water is a delight to drink. Only in the villages and in the wake of foreign expeditions does the dirt and trash accumulate. Man, alas, is the great polluter of his environment—particularly modern industrial man—and because there are few men in the Himalayas, the great mountain slopes have been little harmed and rise in grandeur and beauty.

The summits thrust towards the sky in unbelievable fashion. Massive rock buttresses, unstable ice bulges, clinging snow slopes . . . all piled one on top of the other. Above soar knife-sharp saw-toothed ridges—the final defences before the ultimate summits. They are always changing as the moods of nature change. A bitter wind blows a plume of snow off a lofty mountain brow; sunset transforms the snow and rock to crimson and gold; a fierce storm clothes the mountains in a cloak of purest snow. . . .

As he looks at the mountains the climber's heart swells with joy and pain! It is so beautiful and yet so inaccessible. Oh! to set foot on those virgin slopes—even though death waits poised above!

Why do men want to climb mountains? George Leigh Mallory gave his answer for Mount Everest—"because it is there!" Perhaps there are no cold intellectual reasons—it is more a feeling, a wanting . . . the summit beckons . . . it is impossible, they say . . . impossible? to the spirit of man?—and so the contest is joined! The climber's skill and courage against the defences and dangers of the mountain.

The contest brings fear and joy—and a deep respect. And whatever the result of the struggle—be it success or failure—there is always the desire to go back—yes! to go back. . . .

My friend Yoshikazu Shirakawa has felt the call of the Himalayas just as I have. For three years he has returned again and again to capture on film their serenity, mysticism and grandeur. No one can doubt his love of mountains—his wonderful pictures speak for themselves—and he could not have succeeded in his objective without courage and great determination. With this book Mr. Shirakawa has indeed reached a photographic "Everest."

Edmund Hillary   9

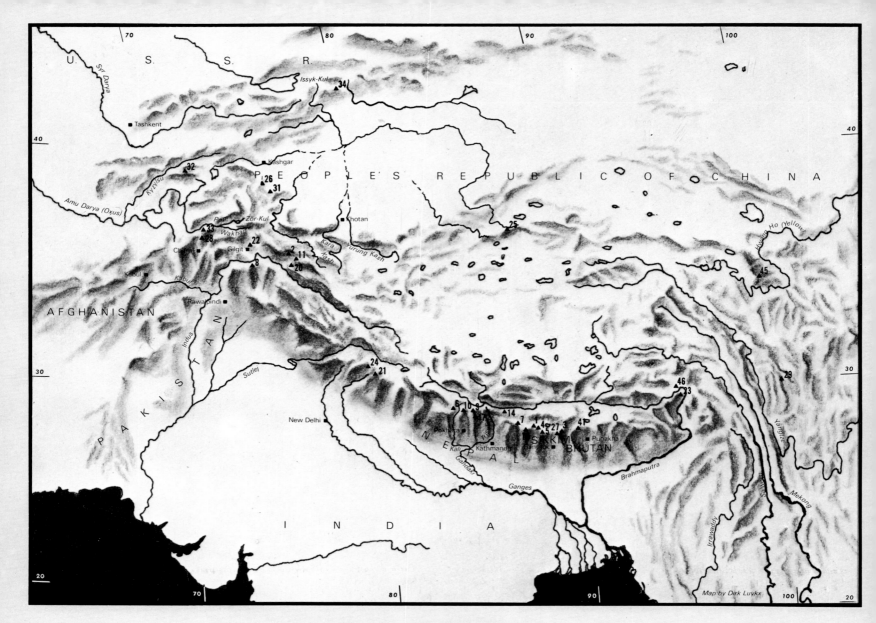

PRINCIPAL PEAKS IN THE HIMALAYAS

No.	Peak	Himalaya Range and Location	Height in Meters	Feet
1.	Everest	Nepal (Nepal-Tibet)	8848	29,028
2.	K2	Karakorum (India)	8611	28,250
3.	Kangchenjunga	Sikkim (Nepal-India)	8598	28,146
4.	Lhotse (highest peak)	Nepal (Nepal-Tibet)	8501	27,891
5.	Makalu	Nepal (Nepal-Tibet)	8475	27,790
6.	Dhaulagiri	Nepal (Nepal)	8167	26,826
7.	Cho Oyu	Nepal (Nepal-Tibet)	8153	26,750
8.	Nanga Parbat	Punjab (India)	8126	26,661
9.	Manaslu	Nepal (Nepal)	8125	26,658
10.	Annapurna (highest peak)	Nepal (Nepal)	8091	26,502
11.	Gasherbrum I (Hidden Peak)	Karakorum (India)	8068	26,470
12.	Broad	Karakorum (India)	8047	26,402
13.	Gasherbrum II	Karakorum (India)	8035	26,363
14.	Gosainthan (Shisha Pangma)	Nepal (Tibet)	8013	26,291
15.	Annapurna II	Nepal (Nepal)	7937	26,041
16.	Kangbachen	Sikkim (Nepal)	7902	25,926
17.	Himaluchuli	Nepal (Nepal)	7892	25,894
18.	Nuptse	Nepal (Nepal)	7879	25,851
19.	Dakura	Nepal (Nepal)	7837	25,713
20.	Masherbrum	Karakorum (India)	7820	25,657
21.	Nanda Devi	Garhwal (India)	7817	25,647
22.	Rakaposhi	Karakorum (India)	7788	25,552
23.	Namcha Barwa	Assam (Tibet)	7756	25,447
24.	Kamet	Garhwal (India)	7756	25,447
25.	Ulug Mustagh	Kunlun (China-Tibet)	7724	25,340
26.	Kungur	Pamir (China)	7719	25,326
27.	Jannu	Sikkim (Nepal)	7710	25,296
28.	Tirich Mir	Hindu Kush (Pakistan)	7706	25,230
29.	Minyag Gongkar	Kunlun (China)	7587	24,893
30.	Changtse	Nepal (Tibet)	7553	24,781
31.	Mustagh Ata	Pamir (China)	7546	24,757
32.	Kommunizma	Pamir (U.S.S.R.)	7495	24,590
33.	Noshaq	Hindu Kush (Pakistan)	7492	24,581
34.	Pobejda	Tien Shan (U.S.S.R.)	7439	24,407
35.	Ganesh Himal	Nepal (Nepal)	7406	24,299
36.	Istor-o-Nal	Hindu Kush (Pakistan)	7403	24,289
37.	Saraghrar	Hindu Kush (Pakistan)	7349	24,112
38.	Talung	Sikkim (Nepal)	7349	24,112
39.	Kabru	Sikkim (Nepal)	7338	24,076
40.	Chamlang	Nepal (Nepal)	7319	24,014
41.	Chomolhari	Bhutan (Bhutan-Tibet)	7314	23,997
42.	Langtang Lirung	Nepal (Nepal)	7245	23,771
43.	Sharphu	Sikkim (Nepal)	7200	23,623
44.	Melungtse	Nepal (Nepal)	7181	23,561
45.	Amne Machin	Kunlun (China)	7160	23,492
46.	Gyari Peri	Bhutan (Bhutan)	7150	23,459
47.	Gaurisankar	Nepal (Nepal-Tibet)	7150	23,459
48.	Pumo Ri	Nepal (Nepal-Tibet)	7145	23,443
49.	Nun Kun	Punjab (India)	7135	23,410
50.	Lenina	Tien Shan (U.S.S.R.)	7134	23,407
51.	Kangto	Assam (India-Tibet)	7090	23,262
52.	Rakhiot	Punjab (India)	7070	23,197
53.	Nupchu	Sikkim (Nepal)	7028	23,052
54.	Khan Tengri	Tien Shan (U.S.S.R.)	6995	22,950
55.	Machapuchare	Nepal (Nepal)	6993	22,944
56.	Lamjung Himal	Nepal (Nepal)	6931	22,741
57.	Siniolchu	Sikkim (India)	6887	22,596
58.	Ama Dablam	Nepal (Nepal)	6856	22,494

Tibet: Autonomous Division of Sikang Province, People's Republic of China

THE
GREAT HIMALAYAS
by Kyuya Fukada

ORIGIN

In the beginning, there were no Himalayas. Between present-day Tibet and India there lay only a vast stretch of shallow sea. The reasons are still not known why the land masses on either side moved toward each other and forced the underwater area upward, but the rising land gradually formed the great range of mountains. Fossils of marine life found 8,000 meters high, while deformed and difficult to recognize, bear out the theory that the Himalayas were once submerged.

I have a small piece of limestone, so soft that one can scratch it with one's fingernail, from Mt. Everest's summit, given to me by Mr. Naomi Uemura, who climbed the mountain on May 11, 1970. The layers of limestone that cover all of Mt. Everest above 8,000 meters, once under water, now lie on a foundation of hard, uplifted rock.

The Himalayas are still rising because the hard earth crust continues to exert pressure from north and south of them. Scientists report that since the end of the last glacial epoch some twenty thousand years ago, the Himalayas have grown 1,500 to 2,000 meters higher. The annual growth rate is 7.5 to 10 centimeters, which means one meter every ten years, ten meters every hundred years. Until fairly recently Mt. Everest's official height was accepted to be 8,840 meters above sea level, the measurement dating from the mid-nineteenth century. Surveys now place the mountain's height at 8,848 meters, an increase of eight meters in approximately one hundred years. Other peaks in the 8,000-meter class, such as Dhaulagiri and Annapurna, all measured from the Ganges Plain in the nineteenth century, have also grown. Mountaineers and all mountain enthusiasts take pleasure in knowing that the Himalayas are steadily growing taller at a time when much of the earth's surface is gradually being eroded by weathering and corrosion.

Rivers provide further evidence that the Himalayas rose from lowlands. Several rivers having their sources in Tibet, for instance, flow between the soaring walls of the Himalayas into the great plains of India, a geographical characteristic that is peculiar to the Himalayas. Deep valleys have been cut through the ranges in many places by rivers that flowed from Tibet before the Himalayas were formed. As the mountains rose, these rivers cut their way across the range from north to south. All the famous rivers of Nepal—the Arun in the east, the Trisuli and Kali in the center, and the Karnali in the west—have formed deep valleys through the main range of the Himalayas. The banks are extremely steep, some rising 4,000 to 5,000 meters straight up from the channel bottoms. The Kali Gandaki River flows between Annapurna and Dhaulagiri at about 1,500 meters above sea level, and the majestic Dhaulagiri towers 8,167 meters, only 6.5 kilometers away. A few more statistics: 4 kilometers from the bed of the Hunza River, 1,800 meters high, is Mt. Rakaposhi at 7,788 meters; 22 kilometers from the Indus River, 1,200 meters high, is Nanga Parbat at 8,125 meters; 13 kilometers from the bed of the Trisuli River, at about 1,800 meters, stands Langtang Lirung at 7,245 meters.

The valleys have long served as trade routes between Tibet and India. Accounts by Himalayan travelers frequently tell of Tibetan traders leading donkeys and sheep laden with salt down these deep valley routes, and of Nepalese merchants going northward with loads of rice. Culture and religion have been exchanged and numerous people have migrated to other lands over these routes.

Between the areas separated by the range there are great differences in climate and vegetation. The south side of the Himalayas is humid, its flora luxuriant, while most areas on the north side are dry and barren. Books about climbing the Himalayas usually begin with accounts of the sweltering heat in India, next of the damp zone with its abundant exotic plants, then the grassy highlands and some of the world's freshest air. The real climbing begins at the foot of the mountains, the piedmont, at an altitude of 4,000 to 5,000 meters. There is no life here; it is a world of snow and ice. After passing through two types of climate, the tropical and subtropical, climbers enter an arctic-like region.

11

EXTENT OF THE HIMALAYAS

"Himalaya" comes from an old Sanskrit word meaning "house of snow." Actually, it combines two words, *him* and *alaya,* the first meaning "snow" and the second "dwelling place." In Buddhist scriptures compiled in Chinese the word appears as either *hsüeh*-ts'ang, "storehouse of snow," or *hsüeh*-chu, "repository of snow," rather faithful renderings of the Sanskrit original. One sees the ancients standing on the plains of India and choosing a name to describe the snow-covered peaks shining magnificently in the north.

The Himalayas are the world's mightiest mountains. No other chain has any mountains higher than 7,000 meters above sea level; the Himalayan range has fourteen peaks over 8,000 meters and hundreds over 7,000 meters. Eight of the tallest are in Nepal and one (Gosainthan, or Shisha Pangma), in Tibet, is near the Nepalese border:

1.	Everest	8,848 meters
2.	Kangchenjunga	8,598 meters
3.	Lhotse	8,501 meters
4.	Makalu	8,470 meters
5.	Dhaulagiri	8,167 meters
6.	Cho Oyu	8,153 meters
7.	Manaslu	8,125 meters
8.	Annapurna	8,091 meters
9.	Gosainthan	8,013 meters

These peaks constitute what we generally call the Himalaya Range, a great arc over 2,700 kilometers long between the Indus River in the west and the Brahmaputra River in the east. At the western end of the arc lies another great range, the Karakorum. There have been disputes as to including this range in the Himalayas: one scholar regards the two as different chains, separated by the upper reaches of the Indus River (more precisely, the Shyok River, a tributary of the Indus); another asserts that neither geographic nor structural differences between the two can be discerned.

It is, in my opinion, only common sense to include the Karakorum among the Himalayas; it was usual in the nineteenth century to speak of the Karakorum Himalayas. With the Karakorum excluded, the stature of the other Himalayas would diminish considerably, for the Karakorum includes four of the highest peaks in the world, each over 8,000 meters. The second highest mountain in the world, K2 (or Mt. Godwin Austen) at 8,611 meters, stands in the Karakorum Range. The other three are: Hidden Peak, 8,068 meters; Broad Peak, 8,047 meters; and Gasherbrum II, 8,035 meters.

West of the Karakorum lies the great range called the Hindu Kush, which has only recently attracted mountaineers. Several peaks soar above 7,000 meters. It is possible to consider this range a part of the Himalayas in the broad sense. The Hindu Kush stands between the Oxus and Indus rivers, once forming the boundary between Central Asia and the Indian subcontinent. Today it is the border between Afghanistan and Pakistan.

The scope of the Himalayas may be extended to include all the high mountains in Central Asia. Given the idea of a "storehouse of snow" and considering the similarities in religions and customs shared by the Asiatic peoples in this vast region, it would not be farfetched to call all these mountains the Himalayas. One standard reference book on the Himalayas, *Sketch of the Geography and Geology of the Himalayan Mountains and Tibet* by Burrard, includes the mountainous areas of Sinkiang in China, the Hindu Kush in Afghanistan, and the Pamir Plateau in Tadzhikistan, U.S.S.R. In this region there are fourteen peaks over 8,000 meters and hundreds over 7,000 meters, including some 200 notable ones. And although mountains over 5,000 meters are rare on other continents, in Central Asia they are so numerous that no one has ever counted them. Many of the great rivers of the world—the Yellow (Hwang Ho), Yangtze, Mekong, Irrawaddy, Brahmaputra, Ganges, Indus, and Oxus (Amu-Dar'ya)—have their headwaters in the Himalayas.

I shall consider the Himalaya Range to extend through eight countries: the U.S.S.R., the People's Republic of China, India, Bhutan, Sikkim, Nepal, Pakistan, and Afghanistan. This area is called the "roof of the world." The Himalayas still preserve many spots unspoiled by man, making the area perhaps the greatest storehouse of secrets in the world. Range upon range of magnificent mountains, snow-clad, their ancient peaks wrapped in mystery and sublime beauty—the Himalayas will never lose their fascination for us.

THE HINDU KUSH

The map entitled *The Himalaya Mountains and Surrounding Regions,* published by the Land Survey Council of India, is on a scale of one to fifteen thousand. It covers the area between longitude 68° and 102° east and latitude 26° to 44° north, the region that contains every mountain in the world over 7,000 meters high. Here the earth's crust made its stupendous skyward thrust.

At the western end lies the Hindu Kush range, divided into western, central, and eastern sections. Toward the east the mountains increase in height: in the Pakistan-Afghanistan border region more than ten peaks are over 7,000 meters high. The four greatest are Tirich Mir, Noshaq, Istor-o-Nal, and Saraghrar. Before 1945 no Hindu Kush mountains had been climbed; many peaks fell in the 1960's, and numerous expeditions have come to these mountains recently. Interest in climbing here developed when other Himalayan countries began to refuse entry to foreign climbers, particularly to the Nepal Himalayas and the Karakorum; besides, the Hindu Kush mountains can be climbed with comparatively light equipment, and the weather in the region is generally less exacting. But some peaks are still untouched, and others, ignored previously as unimpressive mounds of rocks on the ridges of higher mountains, have become ''important'' targets for conquest. Until recently it was thought that the highest peak in the Hindu Kush was Tirich Mir, a mountain already climbed. But the top has now been subdivided into the main peak, the east peak, and west peak I and west peak IV, and each climb of these sub-peaks is carefully recorded.

When defined in this fashion there are nearly two hundred peaks over 6,000 meters in the Hindu Kush; climbs of 145 of them have been backed with authenticated photographs and records. Yet the Hindu Kush mountains have not been thoroughly charted. To take one example: Istor-o-Nal (7,403 meters), one of the four highest peaks, was believed to be the first peak conquered in the range, falling to an American party in 1955. In 1968 four Japanese women reached the same summit, and published an account of their explorations. A mountain buff in Japan, seeing the frontispiece photo, became suspicious: was this really the highest peak of Istor-o-Nal? He gathered information, consulted experts and buffs throughout the world, and became convinced that the party had not reached the summit but a peak west of the top—and that the earlier American party had stood on a lesser peak on the western ridge. The true summit of Istor-o-Nal was climbed by a Spanish party in 1969, the same year of his disclosure.

The western Hindu Kush and a range which runs parallel to it, together called the Hindu Raj sub-range, have begun to attract alpinists. Between the two sections runs the Yarkhun River, which successively becomes the Mastuj, Chitral, and Kunar, and, after meeting the Kabul River, pours into the Indus River. The Hindu Kush and the Karakorum meet at the source of the Yarkhun River.

PAMIR

This area, a vast stretch of high ground called the Pamir Plateau, was the first that geographers named the ''roof of the world.'' The Hindu Kush, after running northward along the Pakistan-Afghanistan border, continues east with the Oxus River. The famous Wakhan Valley is located there. Hsüan-tsang, the distinguished seventh-century Chinese Buddhist monk who traveled to India, and Marco Polo, the thirteenth-century Italian adventurer, are believed to have journeyed up the Oxus River and entered the mountains in Pamir. Both saw Zor-Kul, the beautiful lake near the source of the Pamir River. Hsüan-tsang called it the ''Lake of the Great Dragon,'' and described it as the most splendid spot in the world; the Italian traveler observed the highlands around the lake with the excellent grasses for livestock, and remarked that a thin cow would become fat after grazing in the area for ten days. The wild, crooked-horned sheep in the area today are called Ovis Poli, Polo's sheep.

In 1838 Captain John Wood, an English explorer, rediscovered the lake and named it Lake Victoria. Later, the explorer Sir Mark Aurel Stein was impressed by its placidity and great beauty.

The vast mountainous region between the Pamir and Oxus rivers is the Wakhan Range, having several peaks over 6,000 meters and a number of lesser peaks, none yet climbed. Along the Oxus is the Wakhjir Pass, where the Pamir and Karakorum ranges meet. It usually was across this pass that people entered the Pamir region, or, northward from Gilgit, through the Mintaka or Kilik passes to the Pamir Road. Hsüan-tsang calls Pamir ''Pomiro,'' Marco Polo ''Pamiel.'' Pamir is an old place name.

Silk Road traders and caravans went east into Pamir through the Tash Kurghan Pass and reached Kashgar in Sinkiang-Uighur in China. Kashgar, located at the western edge of the Takla Makan Desert, has been an important town for traders since ancient times. Overlooking it are two lofty peaks, Kungur and Mustagh Ata, both above 7,500 meters. Kungur has two prominent peaks: Kungur I was reached in 1956 by climbers from the U.S.S.R. and the People's Republic of China. A party of Chinese women reached the same summit in 1961; two leaders, native Tibetans, set the altitude record for female alpinists. Kungur II, still unclimbed, is higher. Numerous unclimbed mountains in the hinterland of China are extremely enticing.

Most of the Pamir region belongs to Russia. Between this long mountain range and the great Trans Alai mountains runs the Kyzylsu River. The original Silk Road began at Kashgar, ran westward through the Torugart Pass on the borders of present-day China and Russia, down to the Kyzylsu, and finally to the Oxus River.

The highest mountains in the U.S.S.R. are in Pamir and in the Tien Shan district. The Russians have scaled their highest peaks many times. They have climbed Pik Kommunizma, the highest mountain in Russia, over dangerous variation routes, and hundreds have reached the top of Pik Lenina, Russia's third highest mountain. Surely no other mountain in the world over 7,000 meters has received as many visitors.

THE TIEN SHAN RANGE

Many people confuse Pamir and Tien Shan, even close students of the mountains of Central Asia. The Tien Shan is a long range north of the Pamir, the two roughly divided by an east-west line connecting the Fergana Basin and Kashgar. The Tien Shan makes complicated turns: after moving north from the Pamir it changes its course to run east-west along the border of the Republic of Kirghiz in the U.S.S.R. and the northern edge of the Sinkiang-Uighur region. The mountains take a sharp turn northward from there and then shift almost due east. Away from the border the range gradually flattens, and disappears in the Gobi Desert.

Tien Shan was named by the Chinese during the Han Dynasty; it was not then a high range, for it included only the easternmost part of the present-day range. The North Route and South Route, famous old silk routes, run through the north and south piedmonts of the Tien Shan. Most prominent among the eastern mountains is Bogdo Ula, 5,470 meters high (although the figure is disputed), which must look magnificent from Urumchi, a nearby town only 900 meters above sea level. Small wonder that the mountain is celebrated in old Chinese writings. In 1908 the German explorer Meltzbach climbed Bogdo Ula, and found only steep glaciation near the summit. The peak still defies human approach; in 1949 Shipton and Tilman, noted Himalayan experts, attempted the summit but failed.

The highest peaks are in the central region. Pyotr Petrovich Semyonov, a Russian explorer, entered this area in 1856, via Alma-Ata (now capital of the Republic of Kazakh, U.S.S.R.), and approached Khan Tengri (6,995 meters), the most celebrated mountain in the Tien Shan. (Semyonov so loved the Tien Shan Range that he took on another name for himself, Tienshansky.) *Khan* means "King," and *tengri* means "spirits"; Khan Tengri means something like "King of the Spirits," a suitable name for the mountain long worshiped by people on the south side of the range. Its peak was thought too lofty to climb, and the mountain fell only in 1931 to a Russian party which reached the summit from the Kazakh side after overcoming tremendous difficulties. In 1937 a higher peak than Khan Tengri was discovered and named Pik Pobejda (Peak of Victory; 7,439 meters). This is the next highest mountain in the Soviet Union after Pik Kommunizma.

The Tien Shan, one of the most expansive mountain ranges, has different names according to its sections. The western and central sections, running north along the border between Russia and China, are called the Meridian Range; several sub-ranges extend west like parallel branches into the Soviet Union. These sub-ranges diminish in altitude until the mountains lose themselves in the Kyzyl-Kum Desert.

Between these parallel lines of mountains is the famous Lake Issyk-Kul. Hsüan-tsang reportedly passed it after he crossed the Tien Shan from Sinkiang-Uighur, and called it the Great Clear Lake. The Tien Shan Valley roads have served as silk routes connecting the East and the West. From his capital at Samarkand the army of Timur (Tamerlane) also used these routes in the fourteenth century. Legend tells of an island in Issyk-Kul, now submerged, and of a palace on it built for Timur, the Mongol conqueror. The story could be more than legend, for Russian archeologists have found on the lake bottom remnants of what might be brick walls and water pipes, as well as cooking pots, stone mortars, broken pieces of glass, coins, copperware, and other artifacts of civilization.

The Tien Shan mountains are now closed to foreign mountaineers. When you take off from the airport of Tashkent, in west Turkestan, you see the white crests of these mountains soaring in the east, a breathtaking view.

THE KUNLUN SHAN

The Tien Shan cuts the northern edge of the Takla Makan Desert; the Kunlun Shan borders it in the south. The name *K'unlun* has nostalgic overtones for Orientals, meaning a holy mountain unimaginably high. Like Tien Shan, Kunlun is also an ancient name that appears in China's oldest books, referring generally to all the great mountains in China's west. In the nineteenth century Ferdinand von Richthofen, the great geographer of Asia and the teacher of Sven Hedin, invented the term "Silk Route" and first clarified the topography of the Kunlun Shan. He divided the Kunlun Range into three regions, western, central, and eastern, and considered it the greatest and oldest mountain range in the world. Oddly enough, few of its peaks have ever been climbed.

In Richthofen's classification, the western Kunlun extends between longitude 76° and 89° east, from the eastern edge of Pamir to the south-central border of the Takla Makan Desert. The water from these mountains winds its way down to wet the northern foothills and form lovely oases, connected by the Takla Makan South Road. Hsüan-tsang and Marco Polo surely walked it. The most prosperous oasis city is Khotan, which has a long history. The Yurung Kash (White Jade) and the Kara Kash (Black Jade) rivers, fed by melted snow and ice from the Kunlun Range, meet to form the Khotan River that winds northward until it dries up in desert sand. The beautiful Khotan jade, cherished from ancient times, was originally quarried in the Yurung Kash and the Kara Kash valleys.

The best-known mountains of the Kunlun are those giving rise to these two rivers. This district has several peaks above 7,000 meters that have never been climbed. W. H. Johnson claimed the summit of an unknown peak of 7,000 meters in 1866–67, but his records proved false; his attempt, however, may have been the only climb of any peak in the entire Kunlun Shan. It is difficult to visualize the vastness of the broad and multi-branched Kunlun. In the Arka Tagh, a minor sub-range, maps show a 7,724-meter peak called Ulug Mustagh. This may be a phantom peak, for no photograph of the mountain exists. In one of Sven Hedin's accounts of his explorations in Central Asia a sketch of one mountain is supposed to be Ulug Mustagh, but its existence is still unproven.

The central Kunlun lies between longitude 89° and 104° east. The range becomes wider and many parallel sub-ranges branch out to the north. It strides over Tibet, Tsinghai, Chamdo, Shenhsi, Kansu, and Szechwan, and has several peaks over 7,000 meters. From this vast expanse of mountains flow the great rivers of Asia: the Hwang Ho (Yellow), Yangtze, Mekong, and Salween.

The Kunlun Range has been denuded by erosion and its body largely destroyed. It has no jagged peaks, only round, smooth ridges: judging from its present form, it was once higher and steeper than the Himalayas. The oldest of the great ranges, the stately Kunlun Range stands like a huge monument. According to Richthofen the central Kunlun contains the Bayan Kara and Hsi-ch'ing ranges. There are two prominent peaks: Minyag Gongkar (7,587 meters), conquered by an American party in 1932; and Amne Machin, long a mysterious mountain and once believed to be higher than Mt. Everest. In 1960 a party of Chinese scientists reached the top and established its height as 7,160 meters.

The eastern Kunlun stands between longitude 104° and 113° east. This is the tail end of the Kunlun, made up of a few branch ranges. The low mountains that run east to longitude 118° may be included in the Kunlun Range.

KARAKORUM

The term ''roof of the world'' was originally applied to the Pamir Plateau, believed to be the highest land area in the world. Many of the great ranges in Asia originate here: the Hindu Kush to the west, the Tien Shan to the northeast, the Kunlun to the east, and the Karakorum to the south.

The Karakorum is exceeded only by the Nepal Himalayas in the number of great peaks and the height of its highest peaks. Nineteen peaks exceed 7,600 meters, four of these over 8,000 meters. In addition there are five great glaciers: from west to east they are Batura (58 kilometers), Hispar (61 kilometers), Biafo (59 kilometers), Baltoro (58 kilometers), and Siachen (72 kilometers). These giant glaciers, flanked by sharp icy ridges, move like silver snakes down the Karakorum mountains.

The highest peak in the range is K2, 8,611 meters, the second highest mountain in the world and thus the first in this area to attract mountain climbers. Montgomerie first measured this mountain from a high point near Kashmir in 1857; convinced of its extraordinary height, he called it K2 (Karakorum 2), the mountain's survey number. His calculations proved it the second highest mountain in the world. In 1861, Godwin Austen first stepped onto these virgin glaciers. He closely approached K2's peak and some people wanted to name it Mt. Godwin Austen; others thought it wrong to name it for an individual, and its survey number, K2, became its official name. On reflection, could there be a better choice for this mountain's name?

Fifty years of exploration passed before K2's summit was reached. Six parties repeatedly assaulted the mountain, and several lives were lost. The chosen route was the steep Abruzzi Ridge on the south, named for Duke Abruzzi, cousin of King Vittorio Emanuele III of Italy and the first climber to attempt this icy ridge. Several American parties attempted to conquer K2, each time forced to retreat just below the summit; victory finally came in 1954 to members of an Italian group led by Ardito Desio, heirs to the tradition of Duke Abruzzi.

All four peaks over 8,000 meters are north of Baltoro Glacier, making this glacier the most frequently trodden. After several days of climbing it one reaches a great open space called Concordia, where many glaciers flow together to form the Baltoro. At the far end of Concordia soars a wide-shouldered mountain called Broad Peak (8,047 meters); the glacier divides here, and at the end of the left fork rises the impossibly high summit pyramid of K2. The right fork leads to two other magnificent peaks in the Karakorum over 8,000 meters, Gasherbrum II and Hidden Peak. On the south shore of Baltoro Glacier stand other great peaks: Chogolisa and Baltoro Kangri, which fell to Japanese parties, and Masherbrum and Sia Kangri.

Other Karakorum glaciers have many high, ice-covered peaks rising around them. The north edge of Hispar Glacier is flanked by Khiangyag Kish, the south edge of Diran Peak. To the right of Siachen Glacier is Saltoro Kangri and at the south edge of Batura Glacier is Batura Peak.

As in the other mountain regions in Central Asia, the distinguished peaks in the Karakorum range have been climbed since 1945, when mountaineers from all over the world began to head toward the Karakorum. If the Pakistan government had not recently prohibited climbers from entering the Karakorum, all its peaks might be scaled by now.

The Karakorum differs in many respects from Nepal. There is little greenery, for the area is almost unaffected by the monsoon rains and stays quite dry. Since sherpas are not available for the climbers, either Baltit or Hunza porters must be hired. The inhabitants of this region resemble Caucasians and belong to the Muslim religion, whereas the Nepalese look Oriental and many are Lamaists.

Karakorum is a Turkish word meaning ''black pebbles,'' which hardly describes shining white-clad peaks. There are black rocks at Karakorum Pass, east of the main range; this was an important pass for traders entering Central Asia, and the name for the pass became the name for the range.

PUNJAB

Southeast of the Karakorum another great range extends over 2,200 kilometers. These are the true Himalayas. For convenience we subdivide them from west to east, as follows:

1. Punjab Himalayas
2. Garhwal Himalayas
3. Nepal Himalayas
4. Sikkim Himalayas
5. Bhutan and Assam Himalayas

The highest peak in the Punjab Himalayas is Nanga Parbat; no Himalayan mountain has a climbing history more dramatic. Once called the ''Devil's Mountain,'' it has claimed over thirty lives. The bravest sherpas used to shrink from it. Rising from the highlands near the Indus River, to 8,126 meters, it attracted a party of climbers as early as 1895, led by Alfred F. Mummery, a courageous man with a reputation in Alpine climbing. He discovered too late that the Alps do not compare to the Himalayas; finding no route through the gigantic walls of hard ice that guard the mountain, he finally attempted the Diamir Wall on the western slope. Neither Mummery nor the two Gurkhas with him came down. From the outset, Nanga Parbat's demonic nature was apparent.

The heyday of Himalaya climbing began after World War I, and Nanga Parbat was a main target. In 1932 a German party led by Willy Merkl focused on Rakhiot Glacier on the northern slope: fighting through deep snow carried by the wet monsoon, they reached the ridge above the glacier but could go no higher. Two years later Merkl led a powerful and well-equipped party; advancing on the icy ridge of the same glacier, they passed Silberzacken and reached a snow-covered plateau. The summit was 500 meters above them; success was in their grasp. But the Devil's Mountain defended itself with a violent snowstorm. They had to retreat, and on the way down nine of the party, including the leader, were lost. The German expedition of 1937 suffered an even greater loss. The party's leader, seven climbers, and nine sherpas—the whole force at Camp IV—were buried alive under a terrific avalanche at midnight.

But in 1953 a German and Austrian party led by Karl Herligkoffer, Merkl's foster brother, moved to avenge these deaths on Nanga Parbat. Herman Buhl started alone, at 2:30 A.M. on July 3rd, from Camp V on the ridge above Rakhiot Glacier. He passed Silberzacken and the snow plateau, and by 7 P.M. he had reached the summit. It was dark when he started down, without tent or sleeping bag. Miraculously he survived the night, leaning against a steep, icy cliff. Late the next afternoon he returned exhausted to Camp V, having eaten almost nothing since the day before—a demonstration of superhuman will power.

Nanga Parbat was conquered, but its ice-covered rock walls remained inviting to climbers. In 1962 the next German party attempted Mummery's Diamir Wall. After two trial climbs three men reached the summit, undergoing unbelievable difficulties, but only two came back; the third had slipped and fallen to his death. The next try was made on the Rupar Wall on the south slope. Three reconnaissance expeditions were necessary before this difficult route was climbed in 1970; again one climber fell to his death on the way down. Nanga Parbat is the only Himalayan peak over 8,000 meters that has been climbed by three different routes.

Nun Kun Peak, slightly over 7,000 meters high, is another famous mountain in the Punjab region. Since 1898 it has attracted mountaineers from Britain, the Netherlands, and the United States. Nun's summit was finally reached in 1958 by a Swiss missionary and a French woman climber—a cosmopolitan peak indeed.

GARHWAL

The Garhwal Himalayas are separated from the Punjab Himalayas by the Sutlej River, a tributary of the Indus. From these mountains flow many tributaries of the upper Ganges, like the prongs of a rake. Once a British colony, the Garhwal area was the first part of the Himalayas to be explored and surveyed. No peak is over 8,000 meters, but many of these tempt mountaineers who climb with comparatively light equipment.

The Garhwal's attraction is not dignity but a charm that permits climbers to work slowly to the top of the ice-covered peaks and then descend into beautiful flower-decked valleys. It is the consensus of climbers that only in the Garhwal Himalayas can one combine the beauty of nature with a rigorous climb up a high mountain. But climbing in the Garhwal is no picnic, with its numerous peaks over 7,000 meters high. Kamet Peak, the second highest, was tried ten times before it fell; the eleventh and victorious climb was headed by Frank S. Smythe of Britain. One of his companions to the top, R. L. Holdsworth, wore skis up to the Col at 7,025 meters, the highest altitude at which man had skied until Yuichiro Miura skied down the upper slopes of Mt. Everest in 1970. Holdsworth set another record on the top of Kamet Peak: although certainly very tired, he sat down on the snow and lighted his pipe! Nobody could help but admire him, though one might wonder about the effects on a man of smoking at 7,756 meters. A record, albeit a very strange one!

The highest Garhwal peak is Nanda Devi, 7,817 meters, called the pearl of the Himalayas for its loveliness. The graceful symmetry of its perfect twin peaks thrusting to the sky, the main and the east peaks, is a rare visual treat. T. G. Longstaff, who knows almost everything about these mountains, has praised Nanda Devi, believing no mountain in the world is more beautiful. Such a mountain should be an object of worship, and inhabitants of the region have revered this mountain since ancient times as a dwelling place of the gods. The many routes leading to Tibet through the Garhwal Himalayas once carried heavy traffic, and numerous religions are connected with these mountains. Many Hindus and Buddhists go on pilgrimage to various sacred spots along the upper streams of the Alaknanda River. The names for mountains and passes in the area often have religious meanings: Nanda Devi means "blessed goddess."

Foreign mountaineers charted this mountain at an early date, but Nanda Devi, like Kamet, was slow to yield to them. It is extremely difficult even to approach her foothills, the entrance guarded by long, deep gorges. One party finally crossed these in 1934 and entered the south foothills of the mountain. Two years later the summit was reached by H. W. Tilman and N. E. Odell: Tilman is said to have remarked that Nanda Devi had finally succumbed, that the goddess had been made to bow her proud head, but that he, after the exhilaration of victory, became unaccountably sad. The east peak fell in 1939 to a Polish expedition. Twelve years later Roger Duplat led a French party that planned to attain the main summit and then traverse the four-kilometer summit range to the east peak—an unheard-of plan in the 1950's, when variation routes were only beginning to be used in Himalaya climbing. This brave undertaking had a sad result: Duplat and a companion started for the summit from Camp IV, and were last seen climbing into a dense curtain of mist. His death makes particularly poignant a line from a song he wrote: "If some day I die in the mountains . . ."

The loveliness of the Garhwal Himalayas is unchallenged by the primitive splendor of the Karakorum, the Caucasian grace of the Hindu Kush, or the icy ruggedness of the Nepal Himalayas. Mountains and valleys, forests and meadows, butterflies and flowers—everything is in harmony, producing a supreme sensual pleasure for the mountaineer. And few places in the world are so rich in legend and tradition.

NEPAL

The Garhwal ends at the Kali River; eastward lie the Nepal Himalayas. Nepal had long been closed to foreigners, but even Nepal could not resist progress and opened her doors in 1949. Foreign mountaineers were probably the most delighted of all, for in Nepal stand the world's highest mountains, row upon row. Eight peaks soar above 8,000 meters; twenty exceed 7,500 meters. Part of the Nepal range can be seen from Tibet, but most of it was still uncharted in 1949 and the southern faces were not known. No wonder mountaineers became excited.

A French expedition soon received permission to climb Annapurna, and reached the top in its first attempt, making Annapurna the first Nepalese giant to fall. The success stirred mountaineers the world over. No Himalayan mountain before had fallen in an initial attempt: a mountain was usually scouted one year and climbed perhaps the next, and failures were frequent. Annapurna's great height made the feat all the more spectacular, a milestone in Himalayan climbing. The leader, Maurice Herzog, said they had merely applied techniques used in the European Alps, but their equipment was new: nylon tents and ropes, boots with synthetic rubber soles, tools and utensils of lightweight metal alloys. The Annapurna expedition was highly innovative, and its success undoubtedly lay in the quick Alpine-style attack with light gear. The price for victory was dear, however; the two who reached the summit became severely frost-bitten and blinded by snow. After they were rescued, they had to be carried down on stretchers. In the hospital Maurice Herzog wrote an exciting book about the conquest of Annapurna, ever popular among mountain lovers.

This was the beginning of the climbs on mountains over 8,000 meters. Men from all countries began competing for the superpeaks, leading to the expression "the Himalayan Olympics." The British aimed for Everest: they had been defeated in seven previous attempts, for climbs had to be up the north slope from Tibet before the approach from Nepal was opened. The situation was reversed in 1949: Nepal could be entered but not Tibet. A scouting party sent to the south slope chose a route above Khumbu Glacier. Climbers in the Himalayas frequently "stand on their predecessors' shoulders"; a Swiss party almost made the summit in 1952, following the route the British had just discovered; in 1953 the British party succeeded, benefiting from the Swiss experiences. The names of Edmund Hillary and Tenzing Norkay spread throughout the world.

The decade after Annapurna can be called the Golden Age of Himalaya mountaineering. Fourteen peaks over 8,000 meters in the Himalayas, including the Karakorum, fell to parties from Austria, England, France, Germany, Italy, Japan, Switzerland, and the United States. Certain mountains in Nepal proved stubborn: Dhaulagiri resisted challenges by expeditions from France, Switzerland, Argentina, Germany, and Austria before falling to the Swiss in 1960. One unconquered peak over 8,000 meters was Gosainthan, in Tibetan territory, accessible only to climbers from the People's Republic of China. The Chinese sent a scouting party in 1963, and in 1964 organized an enormous 195-member expeditionary party (the number, which may surprise westerners, includes porters as well as regular members). The plan was to reach the top of Shisha Pangma (Gosainthan's Tibetan name) on May Day 1964, and they missed by just one day; ten persons reached the summit on May 2nd, and fifty-three the slope below, 7,500 meters high.

VARIATION ROUTES

All the Himalayan peaks over 8,000 meters have now been conquered, and almost all of those over 7,000 meters; few high mountains in the Nepal Himalayas have not been approached. Knowledge and experience in Himalaya climbing are now so plentiful that no peak is impregnable.

In the Alps no unclimbed peaks remain. Before rock-climbing came into vogue, climbing variation routes was practiced, perhaps the hardest way to climb a mountain. Climbing in the Nepal Himalayas seems to be following that example. Nor had traversing a mountain—going up by one route and coming down by another—been tried in the Himalayas until 1963, when traversing was first undertaken on Mt. Everest.

Most Himalaya climbers care only for unclimbed peaks, but Mt. Everest, the highest mountain in the world, is hard to resist: since the British success in 1953, Everest's top has been reached a number of times. Each party has added to the technique of climbing Everest. The Swiss, the second party, reached the summits of Everest and Lhotse almost simultaneously. The third party was Chinese; they are believed to have used the Tibetan route, unsuccessfully attempted several times by the British. The Americans, the fourth party, accomplished something new—traversing: two climbers reached the top along the classic route from the southeast ridge; two others attained the summit via the steep western ridge, and crossed the summit toward the southeast ridge. It was dusk; the plan had been for all four to rendezvous on the summit, but the first team had already started back down the southeast ridge, believing the attempt from the west had failed. In the dark the western team headed down the southeast ridge and caught up with their companions, all four men overjoyed at the unexpected meeting. Ahead of them lay the dangerous climb down the steep, narrow ridge in pitch darkness, their oxygen spent and their only flashlight running down; they could only huddle together on a bare platform of icy rocks, spending the night at 8,500 meters without tent, sleeping bags, oxygen, or light. Three were suffering from severe frost-bite when they finally rejoined the rest of their companions.

The fifth party, an Indian group, was determined to succeed in 1965, having failed twice previously. With no ambition to set any record, they hoped to ensure success by organizing four teams to aim simultaneously for the summit. But inadvertently they did set a record, nine members standing at one time on Everest's summit. In 1970 a Japanese party planned to climb via the now-classic route with one team and with another to scale the south wall, the gigantic, perpendicular wall of ice-covered rocks on the southwestern slope of Mt. Everest! The wall drops 2,150 meters straight down to the Western Cwm, where the base camp was set up; above 8,000 meters the wall is vertical, with frightening overhangs. The plan was ambitious, but not reckless; the previous year scouting parties, sent out before and after the monsoon season, had become convinced that the south wall was not impregnable. The two groups included thirty-nine regular members, seven sherpas, seventy-nine members to work above the base camp, and some thousand porters; equipment and food weighed thirty tons; expenditures were the largest ever for a Himalayan expedition. The southeastern group reached the summit. Those on the south wall reached 8,000 meters and gave up in the face of constant falling rocks, yet their attempt stimulated mountaineers throughout the world.

In 1970 a British party attempted the south wall of Annapurna. They had tried a variation route in 1969, climbing to Glacier Dome, then turning west to reach Roc Noir; after conquering the front peak they attempted to follow the 7.5-kilometer ridge to the main peak, but had to quit halfway. In their 1970 expedition they scrambled up the steep south wall directly to the main summit—terribly difficult rock-climbing—and succeeded, but at the cost of one member's life. Also noteworthy in 1970 was a Japanese climb of Makalu, which they had climbed previously but this time by a variation route along the long southeast ridge, succeeding after a painstaking struggle. Perhaps future notable climbing achievements in Nepal will be made over variation routes.

SIKKIM, BHUTAN, ASSAM

East of the Nepal Himalayas lie the Sikkim Himalayas. Exploration in this area began quite early, as it did in the Garhwal Range, but today mountain climbing is forbidden in Sikkim. On the Nepal–Sikkim border is Kangchenjunga, the world's third highest mountain. Before World War II, Darjeeling, in the northeast corner of India, was held sacred by those who loved the Himalayas. From the surrounding hills one looked directly up at the soaring peaks of Kangchenjunga; this fortunate location made the mountain famous long before others were known, and Kangchenjunga was the earliest Himalayan mountain to be explored. Many mid-nineteenth-century scientists and explorers visited the region, but none dreamed of climbing Kangchenjunga's rugged summit. The first to consider it was Douglas Freshfield, who traveled around its base to estimate the dangers and chances for success. In 1905 he attempted Yalung Glacier on the southwest slope, but failed to get far. More determined assaults began with two German parties in 1929 and 1931, each attempting the long northeast ridge above Zemu Glacier on the east slope. But the monsoon season brought snows and terrible storms, and both times they retreated. G. O. Dyhrenfurth organized an international expedition in 1930, which tried Kangchenjunga Glacier on the north slope; when they realized that to advance would be to risk a dangerous avalanche, they had to retreat.

Kangchenjunga appeared impregnable, with no feasible routes. Nevertheless, the mountain finally fell to the British; following scouting expeditions in 1952 and 1954, they chose Yalung Glacier and on May 25th and 26th, 1955, two parties of two men each reached the summit. They stopped short of the highest point, keeping their promise to local authorities to leave untrodden the sacred part of the holy mountain.

The mountain group around Kangchenjunga is vast. Toward Sikkim in the east is Siniolchu, a most beautiful mountain; toward Nepal in the west is Jannu, called ''the monster mountain'' from its grotesque appearance. It had been thought impregnable because it looked so formidable, but in 1959 a French party succeeded after three fierce assaults.

East of the Sikkim lie the Bhutan Himalayas, and further east the Assam Himalayas. The Bhutan and Assam mountains are the least known of the Himalayan chain; both Bhutan and Assam refuse to admit mountaineers. Chomolhari is more appropriately considered Tibetan than Bhutanese. As one enters the village of Phari Dzong, by the old road leading through Sikkim to Tibet from India, one suddenly faces Mt. Chomolhari in its splendor, and all travelers have words of praise for it. In Tibetan *cho* means God, *mo* is a feminine suffix, and *lhari* means a holy mountain: Chomolhari, "the holy mountain of the Goddess," has been worshiped as such by the Tibetans. It was scaled from the Tibet side in 1937 by a British party: Spencer Chapman and a friend, aided by three sherpas, succeeded with almost no money and using borrowed equipment. No one has done so since.

Few mountaineers have entered the Assam Himalayas. In 1939 Tilman attempted to climb Mt. Kangto, but reached only a lesser mountain on the approach. The mountains in Assam are guarded by dense jungle areas between the villages and the mountains; it rains a great deal in the region; a deadly illness is rampant. But the main obstacle today is rather the political difficulties with the Chinese concerning the border. At the far eastern end of the Assam Himalayas stands Namcha Barwa, 7,756 meters, discovered in 1912, the last high peak in the approximately 2,700-kilometer-long Himalayas. Gyara Peri, 7,150 meters, was discovered in 1913, just across the Brahmaputra River. Namcha Barwa and Gyara Peri will occupy the thoughts of Himalaya mountaineers for a long time to come.

REGIONAL MAPS

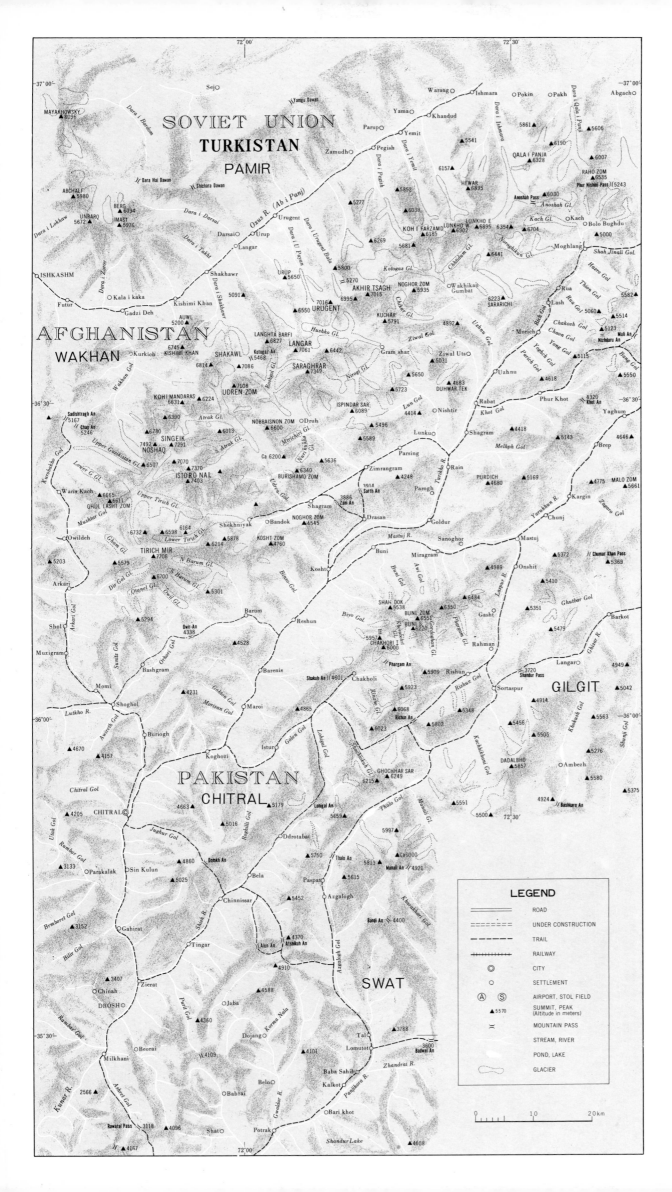

HINDU KUSH AREA

Edited by Tsuneo Miyamori

LEGEND

═══════	ROAD
════════	UNDER CONSTRUCTION
─ ─ ─ ─	TRAIL
+++++++	RAILWAY
◎	CITY
○	SETTLEMENT
Ⓐ Ⓢ	AIRPORT, STOL FIELD
▲5570	SUMMIT, PEAK (Altitude in meters)
╳	MOUNTAIN PASS
	STREAM, RIVER
	POND, LAKE
	GLACIER

0   10   20km

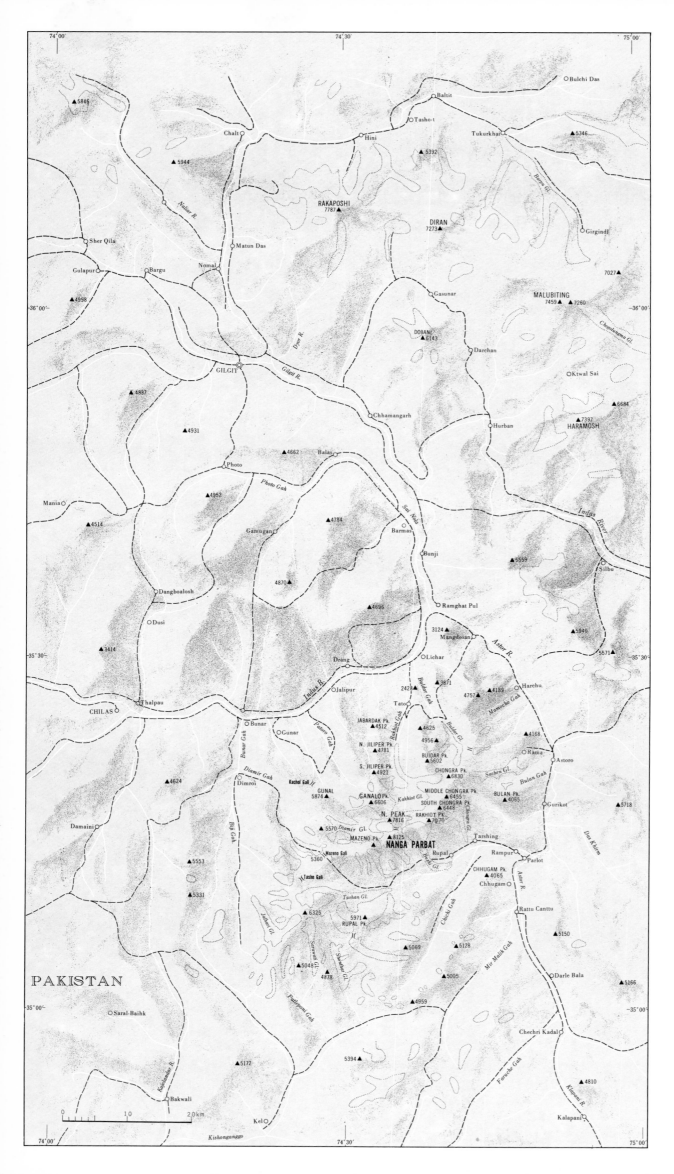

NANGA PARBAT AREA

Edited by Tomoya Iozawa

◄

ANNAPURNA AREA

Edited by Tomoya Iozawa

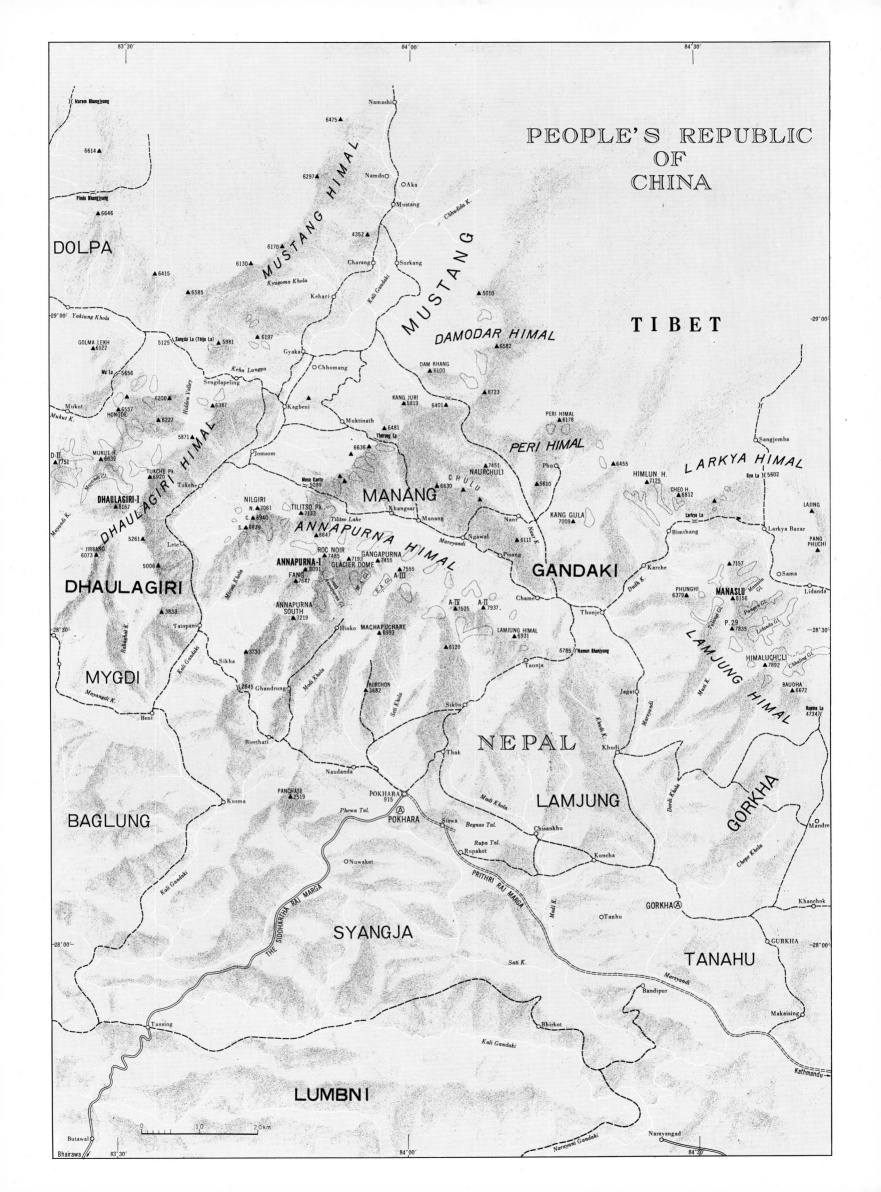

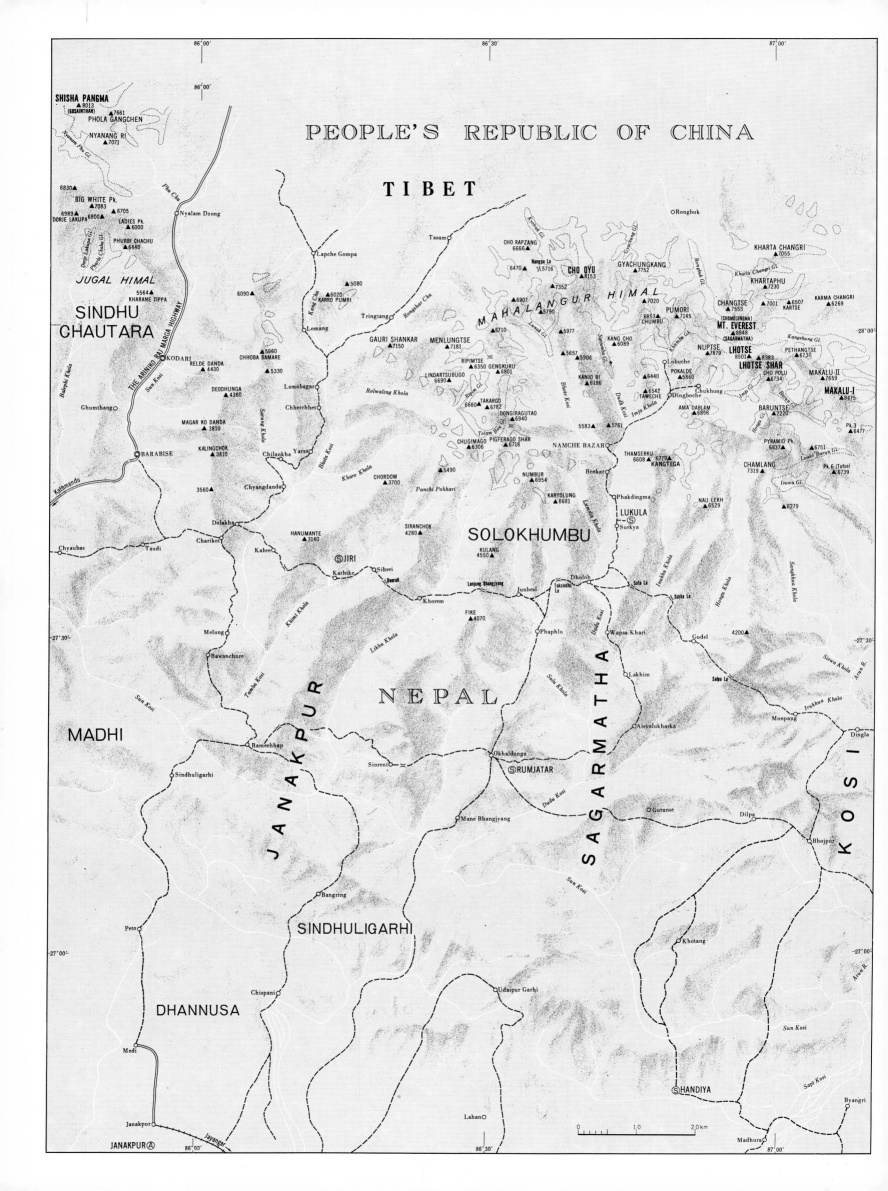

EVEREST
AREA

Edited by Tomoya Iozawa

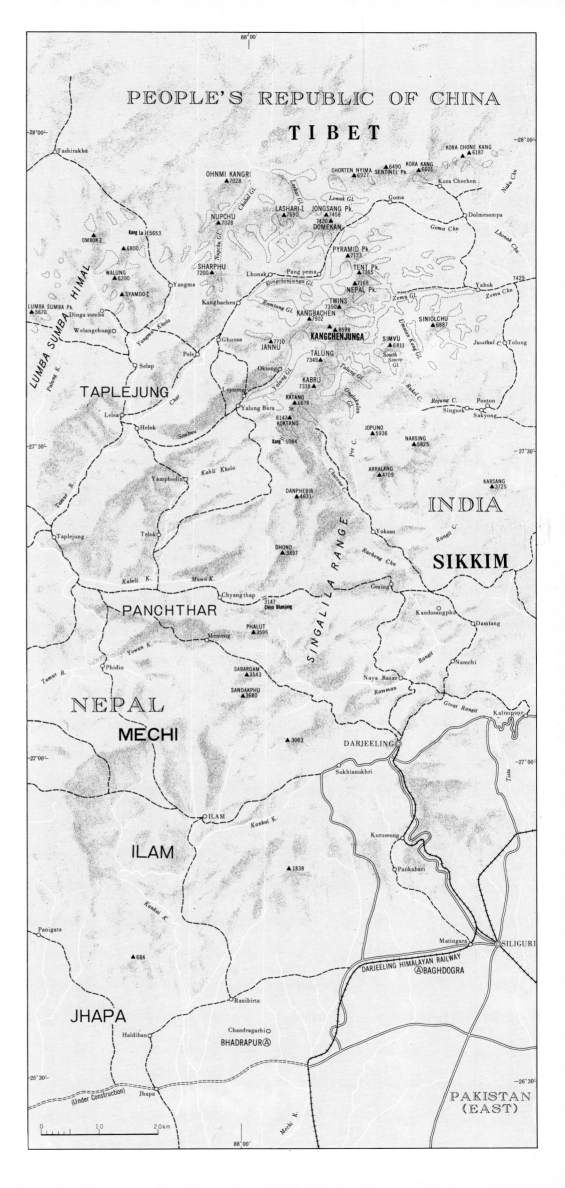

KANGCHENJUNGA

AREA

Edited by Tomoya Iozawa

NEPAL HIMALAYAS

PUNJAB HIMALAYAS

The Nepal Himalayas

EVEREST AND VICINITY (see map, page 24)

Nepal ended a long period of national isolation in 1949. The first foreign visitors were a French climbing party that attacked Annapurna I, and on June 3, 1950, they became the first to reach its summit. The news of their feat, so soon after the opening of Nepal, excited many climbers; within ten years every mountain over 8,000 meters in Nepal had fallen, an astounding accomplishment.

Nepal contains more high peaks than any other section of the Himalayas. Near Everest rise Makalu, Lhotse, and Cho Oyu, all over 8,000 meters, and I began my Himalayan photography expedition here. From Kathmandu we flew to Lukula (Plate 1), a distance that would have taken twelve days by foot. The climb would have accustomed us gradually to thinner air and prevented our later mountain sickness, but I had no patience; thinking "time is money" and "the sooner the better," I hurried over the mountains by chartered helicopter. Our party included myself, two assistants, and three sherpa porters; photography equipment, climbing supplies, and food made 400 kilograms of baggage. In Lukula I hired additional porters and we set off that day for Namche Bazar, arriving two days later. It was still daytime, but when the tent was pitched I lay down at once and slept, a clear sign of mountain sickness.

I photographed mountains around Thamserku the next day (Plates 22, 24), then flew to Thyangboche, the site of a large Lama monastery. Our arrival coincided with their New Year, and noisy festivities were in full swing. In the mountains such merrymaking is rare, and many people had traveled there from far. We joined in, and even met the Head Monk of the lamasery. The sherpas prostrated themselves while they were in his presence, remaining motionless until he left. After photographing the festival for two days we moved on to the village of Dingboche, where two routes diverge: one leads across Khumbu Glacier to Everest's Base Camp, the other goes over Chukhung to Lhotse Glacier. That night one of my assistants had not arrived. It was growing dark, so I sent out to look for him; he had collapsed in the snow, our first victim of mountain sickness, so weak he could barely speak. A porter carried him back to the camp. That night was freezing cold, with fierce wind.

We flew deeper into the mountains by helicopter, and again began ascending by foot. Aware of the danger of mountain sickness, we had planned to acclimatize while climbing near Chukhung. I was fallen sick before we reached Dingboche, at 4,000 meters, but we had to establish Base Camp during good weather. The sherpas warned that an avalanche would delay us two or three weeks, since our small party could not clear away the snow. I decided we would take the course up the southern rampart of Mt. Pumo Ri; we might be stricken with mountain sickness, but there was no other choice. So we camped in Dingboche three days, to acclimatize and to impress upon the sherpas the importance of my work. If I fell ill, the photography must still have priority. Taking pictures is my life as well as my profession; I repeated the same words again and again to the sherpas, even making them promise to care for the camera equipment if I died.

We then went up Khumbu Glacier and reached Lhotse. Though I felt weak, we forced on to Gorak Shep. There is no shelter, only a small clearing on the glacier. I have no memory of the place, though I recall in detail the scenery and the faces at the other campsites of my Himalayan explorations; in fact, I remember little until we returned to Lobuche. To view Mt. Everest from the front, we climbed from Gorak Shep up to Kala Pattar on the south side of Pumo Ri, itself a breathtakingly beautiful mountain. The sherpas tell me I photographed Everest twice, once from Kala Pattar and one evening shot from Pumo Ri's summit, but I only remember the latter. Nor do I remember four porters carrying me in turns down from Kala Pattar, though I recall the pain of the rope cutting into my buttocks. And from some boulder-strewn place I photographed Everest and Nuptse at sunset, flaming red in a cloudless sky (Plate 12). Though I was half conscious, our descent to camp impressed my mind indelibly:

struggling slowly down a huge icy slope, leaning on others and guided by flashlights; the lights of camp shining in the darkness ahead; porters and kitchen boys running toward us carrying flashlight or lantern and crying "Sahib, Sahib." They threw their arms around me; their relief and happiness at my safe return buoyed my exhausted spirits. That evening I had almost no appetite. I swallowed soup and rice gruel, but my cup and spoon fell from my fingers no matter how firmly I tried to grasp them. Symptoms of mountain sickness include lethargy and loss of muscular control. The next morning I saw that my watch, a most reliable one, had stopped at 1:00 A.M.: I must have tossed in my sleep. My right thumb and forefinger were burned, and many burnt matches were on the floor. Possibly I had tried to light a candle when the intense cold made breathing difficult.

It was plain that illness had begun to affect my thinking. In the mountains a leader's commands are law, and errors in judgment have led to countless tragedies. Immediately I gave orders to descend. Crossing the glacier I frequently stumbled and fell; the porter who carried my baggage to Lobuche returned to carry me. Barely conscious, I took only a few pictures of the magnificent scenery I had dreamed of so long. We stopped two nights at Gorak Shep before continuing down. Once acclimatized, we found our going was easier, and during the next three years I flew the 3,000-kilometer length of the Himalayas many times without distress, even climbed in the Sikkim Himalayas.

Mountain sickness is quite dangerous; if complicated by pneumonia, it can be fatal within forty-eight hours. Over fifty climbers have died from it in the Himalayas. At Dingboche I was startled at my appearance in a mirror. My face was ashen, swollen twice its normal size, and carved with countless tiny deep wrinkles.

From Dingboche we went to Chukhung Glacier. The gigantic 8,501-meter crest of Lhotse rose sharply, seemingly within reach of my hand (Plate 11). Ice towers like glittering suits of armor rose on the front of the glacier, resplendent in the sunlight.

Several nights after we began climbing again, the sherpas were talking in whispers around the fire. When I asked what had happened they told me the *yeti,* the Abominable Snowman, had been sighted, running below an ice tower on Chukhung Glacier toward Ama Dablam. They accepted its existence and their conversation was serious. As I joined them around the fire I began to feel an eerie chill. The Abominable Snowman looks like a small man but has superhuman strength, they said, capable of felling a yak with a single blow. It rips off yaks' legs with its bare hands and carries them into the mountains. It usually appears in the area around Chukhung and Gokyo, right where we were (Plates 3, 9).

For three days Chunkhung was hidden in fog. The Abominable Snowman is said to bring bad weather, and the fog made the sherpas' talk more believable. It became our sole topic of conversation; my assistant swore he had heard its voice in the night, even imitating the sound for us, and grew indignant when I said that mountain sickness had gone to his head. He attached a long-distance lens to his 35mm camera and vowed to photograph the Snowman, keeping his camera with him even at meals. I myself began to feel rather strange. Gazing at the dense fog in the evenings, I found myself half expecting the Abominable Snowman to appear.

When the weather lifted, the sherpas and porters left to track the Snowman, crossing from Imja Glacier to Chukhung Glacier; my assistant hunted for a week, even injuring his leg in the process. But their efforts were useless. We went back to Dingboche, and entered Gokyo on the Ngojumba Glacier, where there were more rumors about the Abominable Snowman, but no one bothered to look for it.

At Gokyo I photographed Everest, Cho Oyu, Gyachung Kang, Taweche, and Cholatse, and the ancient, mysterious Ngojumba Glacier. We returned to Lukula via Namche Bazar. In Kathmandu we had arranged for a helicopter to meet us at Lukula on our return. It was good to see it arrive on schedule.

KATHMANDU BASIN

I photographed the Kathmandu Basin late in 1969, my assistants preceding me and choosing the route we would follow. The photographic expedition went well. Nagarkot is a fine spot in the Kathmandu area for photographing the Himalayas. The mountains look most majestic. All the outstanding peaks, from Dhaulagiri to Makalu, are visible, and one sees famous mountains—Gaurisankar, Cho Oyu, Nuptse, Everest, Lhotse, and other giants. Gosainthan's south wall is almost directly frontal. Damang Pass is another excellent location, though the mountains are quite far away. Kakani Hill, on the other hand, disappointed me; one can see only three peaks of Ganesh Himal.

The best spot for viewing the Himalayas in their entirety, however, is the summit of Chandra Gil, south of Darjeeling (Plate 17). Inaccessible by jeep, the spot requires a four-hour ascent in climbing shoes but the reward is a bird's-eye view of Kathmandu backed by all the Himalayas, from Annapurna to the Everest group. Walking about the Chandra Gil area is exhilarating. We carried a portable stove and cooked our afternoon meal there at the top—a most enjoyable one-day trip.

FROM POKHARA TO ANNAPURNA (see map, page 23)

Many people call Pokhara the most beautiful spot on earth. The surroundings unfold like a screen that no painter could duplicate. Machapuchare, resembling the Matterhorn enough to be its twin, thrusts up into the sky directly before you (Plate 16); to left and right the Annapurna Range stretches so far that you must turn your head to encompass the whole scene. I have viewed the Matterhorn from the Zermatt side, and cannot say which view is finer. In sheer majesty Pokhara surpasses Zermatt, and the numerous lakes contribute to Pokhara's beauty (''Pokhara'' means ''lake'' in the local dialect). But in elegance, in purity of air, and in the rustic charm of the villages, the visual splendors of Pokhara and Zermatt are equal.

We camped in a grass field near the Royal Villa in Pokhara, on the shore of a lake a short distance from Pokhara Airport. The morning and evening beauty of the Annapurna Range was indescribable (Plate 14). Based at Pokhara, we traveled west through Gorapani Pass, up the Kali Gandaki as far as Jomosomba (Plate 2), and east through Imankaluka—ahead of Thonje—as far as Namun Bhanjyang.

Pokhara is in the lowlands and in March it is like summer. Agricultural products are plentiful and there is none of the pathos of the Everest region, where people eke out a living from the frozen land. I was surprised to find oranges growing in the area between Tatopani and Dahna that greatly resembled the mandarin oranges native to Japan.

AERIAL PHOTOGRAPHY

None of the seven countries of the Himalayas officially permits aerial photography. India and Pakistan even forbid photography during commercial flights over flatlands. You can charter a plane and head for the mountains, but you might be caught on a military radar screen and be chased or shot down by fighters. The mountains bordering India and Pakistan are being fortified as the front lines between the two countries, and the national defense policies of both countries forbid all mountain photography; aerial photography is unthinkable.

Nepal's relations with China, however, are friendly. Nepal does not officially permit aerial photography, but permission, if granted, originates as a special consideration of His Royal Highness, the King of Nepal, and all aerial photography is made from the king's private plane. I sat in the co-pilot's seat on the left side of the plane, a sixteen-passenger Twin Otter with jet-prop engines. The Twin Otter is far superior to light planes such as the Piper Cub or Cessna, which do not fly above 4,000 to 5,000 meters, not high enough for Himalayan passes, let alone the mountains; with a high-climbing plane one can penetrate deep into them. We usually flew at 6,000 and 8,000 meters, although I took most of my photographs between 7,000 and 7,500 meters. Oxygen was required above 5,000 meters. This caused us certain troubles, for the king's Twin Otter was not designed for high-altitude flying; its cabin was not sealed and its oxygen equipment did not meet the requirements of sustained flights at the heights I wanted. We had two small tanks, each providing an hour's oxygen for one person and meant to serve only the pilot. From climbing at high altitudes I was somewhat acclimated to thin air, and was usually so engrossed in my work that I hardly bothered about oxygen. But sometimes I became groggy and dropped my camera, even when I thought I held it tight in both hands, and when I bent to pick it up I invariably hit my head against the cockpit window. At such times I was half awake, half asleep; when the pilot saw me he would yell that he was going to fly lower; I yelled for him to fly higher—the mountains around us were 8,000 meters high and if we flew lower my photographs would be worthless. As I slowly lost consciousness I felt as if my stomach was filling with oil and little by little the oil was coming up my throat. When everything turned black my assistant hurriedly fed me enough oxygen to perk me up again. The short oxygen supply meant that we did not employ a co-pilot; two men using oxygen while we flew above 5,000 meters would halve our photographing time. Of the three men aboard, my assistant was acclimated to thin air and required only one minute of oxygen every twenty minutes even at altitudes above 7,000 meters. He was a life-saver, making more flying time available for photography.

The first time we flew to Mt. Everest we bungled our oxygen allotment. Unaccustomed to the equipment, we used up both tanks before arriving on location to start taking pictures. At 8,000 meters with no oxygen, the pilot dropped quickly to a safe altitude and we returned to Kathmandu, sadder and wiser. After that my assistant looked solely after the oxygen equipment when we flew: it took priority over the cameras, the film, and everything else. We ran out of oxygen another time near Makalu. My work was going well, and I wanted to finish; the pilot gave me more time, even though it was extremely dangerous for him to fly without oxygen where rough air currents tossed the airplane about. Near high mountains a pilot needs constant oxygen to keep his head clear, but he kept flying on; I was groggy and slipping toward unconsciousness, alternately seeing and then not seeing the mountains around us. To wake myself up I bit the back of my right hand and the low air pressure caused blood to gush out and splash the window. More than the pain, the sight of the blood brought me to my senses, and I completed my photographing. Two days later we flew to Everest again. As we went higher my bitten hand started swelling; at 7,000 meters blood spurted out again. My head was completely clear, however, and I did not want to waste time tending to my hand; I tried to bandage it with a film case wrapping but could not stop the blood.

My aerial photography ended with three days of flying in the Pokhara area. We made two tanks of oxygen last the whole time, but the work was the hardest of all. I had planned it so we would be near Pokhara when I finished. To photograph Manaslu at sunset, for example, we headed toward Annapurna II or Machapuchare just before actual sundown and shot our final photos (Plate 14). The descent from 8,000 meters takes time; at sunset, the Pokhara area below was already dark. The instant I finished I yelled to the pilot, who immediately dropped down to find Pokhara Airport: ''airport'' is an exaggeration, for it was a grass field with no lights; if we did not land quickly we might never land, and the air strip was pitch dark. Our landing lights were on but we had several high bounces before settling down, the plane angled far to one side.

29

One can only appreciate the awesomeness of the Himalayas from the air (Plates 6, 23). From the ground you cannot usually see the true summits, especially while climbing, yet the summits are the most characteristic parts of these tremendously high mountains. A mountain like Taweche, in the 6,000-meter class, looks nondescript from the ground; from the air its 300-meter-long summit is a giant razor's edge of ice. (Plate 15). Numerous Himalayan mountains are impregnable. In comparison, Everest is a highly climbable mountain; seen from the air Everest is big, very big, but it is a stocky mountain, and with oxygen one can climb it.

I took my aerial photographs from the middle of March to the middle of May. During those two months the mountains' summits changed greatly. From the air one could see that the techniques and energy needed to climb the Himalayas in March, when their peaks were more pointed because of ice, differ from those needed in May.

We tried several times to fly along the north side of the Lamjung Himal, but air currents chased us away (Plate 5). Our last attempt was early one morning: as we approached the area our craft began to shake as though someone were playing with it, and rattled as loudly as machine-gun firing. I saw the pilot's face blanch as he swung the plane toward a cloudless area. Twice we tried to fly between Makalu and Kangtega, but both times we were shaken violently and had to turn away (Plate 8). The topography evidently causes turbulence in both areas.

LIFE WITH THE SHERPAS

We all began to look alike, Japanese and sherpas. Baths are out of the question in the mountains, one cannot even sponge oneself off properly. In time I became used to mountain goat meat, at first unbearably pungent. At 3,700 meters there were no wild chickens, and goats were our only source of protein. One goat lasted our party five days. At first we all watched the beheading process: one sherpa fastened a rope to the animal's horns and pulled; when the goat balked, sticking its neck out, another sherpa delivered the death blow with the *kukri,* a local axe, which is a rather dull-edged tool and requires a powerful swing to do the job in one stroke. The animal's body fell to the ground with a thud: it amazed me that a little goat fell so heavily. The decapitation scenes left me with no appetite at first, and a generous portion of goat hair was often mixed with the meat at dinnertime, but before long I was used to it and ate without grumbling. Food, water, fuel, and other supplies are precious when climbing, and I could not complain that the meat was not washed thoroughly before cooking. Goat soup was delicious. Our cook put a large bone with meat clinging to it into a pan of salted water and simmered it slowly. For variety he sometimes added a little curry, which was also good. Nothing could compare with our dinners, chewing on meaty bones and drinking savory goat broth. When we passed from Pokhara through Annapurna, we were on lower ground and chicken was plentiful, one for each man's meal. I photographed the chickens strutting around before mealtime: those that squawked most vigorously before their necks were wrung proved firm and delicious; those that put up no struggle were less appetizing.

While we photographed the Annapurna Himalayas, one of our campsites was in Gorapani Pass. Our best shots of Machapuchare and Dhaulagiri were taken from the mountaintop above the pass (Plate 10). To take early morning photographs we had to complete all preparations before sunrise, so we told the sherpas to get us up at four A.M.—not an early hour, for we often rose at one or two in the morning. I had been asleep for what seemed a short time when a voice outside the tent called me for breakfast. It was dark; my watch said nine, but I ate breakfast anyway. I asked the time of the two sherpas, and neither had a watch—for two months they had never known the time, but had always been up at the hour I set! The sherpas tell time by the stars and by changes in the color of the eastern sky, and that night was the first they had misjudged; after breakfast I went back to bed for another six hours' sleep. I once asked the sherpas to clean our cooking pans, and did not check on them; they were still polishing the pans that night, having polished them all day. Their simplicity and their sense of responsibility were impressive.

How strong is the sherpas' sense of responsibility is clear from their acts on Nanga Parbat and K2. On Nanga Parbat, the sherpa Geh Reh chose to stay on a ridge facing certain death with the leader of a foreign climbing expedition rather than leave and save himself. His contract did not call for him to die for one of the climbers; his death was a humane act, beyond any impersonal obligation. Pasang Kikuli was another sherpa who showed the utmost devotion and courage on K2. His death also belongs to the pages of Himalayan mountain-climbing history and will be related forever as a story of human devotion. Recent visitors to the Himalayas say that some sherpas have changed from their forefathers, that they are more sophisticated and clearly not of the same fiber.

I remember each sherpa and porter who accompanied me in my Himalayan travels, particularly Gartzen, my chief porter, who was with me for eight months. When I complimented him his face would beam with bashful joy, and when I yelled at him he would look downcast and glance at me sideways with reproachful eyes. Sometimes I suddenly seem to see Gartzen again, carrying seventy pounds of baggage on his back for one dollar a day, trudging silently, sweat dripping from his forehead. I have left friends without a word and returned home alone, when Gartzen came to my mind.

I spent three years trekking the Great Himalayas. My trials in India and Pakistan I will never forget; if I could return to the Himalayas I would go only to Nepal, and without a camera. I would call together the sherpas and porters who worked with me and go with them for a pleasant walk in the mountains. If they knew I was coming they would greet me at Kathmandu Airport, all grinning, and all wearing the same worn-out gym shoes.

The Punjab Himalayas

Leaving its source in the highlands of Tibet, the Indus River cuts through the Kashmir Plateau and flows northwest. Before reaching Gilgit it curves, and flows southward through Pakistan. To the north lies the Karakorum; to the west the Hindu Kush; to the south are the Punjab Himalayas, also called the Kashmir Himalayas. The range extends eastward to the Sutlej River. Within the Punjab Range the treacherous Nanga Parbat (8,125 meters) and Nun Kun (over 7,000 meters) lord it over the other mountains, none so notable as these.

India and Pakistan dispute possession of this region. Under the British, Kashmir was one of India's 562 political units. When India and Pakistan gained independence in 1947, Kashmir became independent, but strong intervention by the Nehru government caused Kashmir to affiliate herself with Hindu India. Since most people in Kashmir are Muslim, a basically religious struggle arose between India and Pakistan; the dispute is less intense today, though not yet ended.

The Kashmir border is hard to determine, the political boundaries being unstable and the *de facto* border a cease-fire line. It was my observation that Nanga Parbat is under Pakistan rule and Srinagar, 120 kilometers south, is under Indian. The entire region was occupied by soldiers, and permission was difficult for climbing mountains, let alone taking pictures.

THE INDIAN SIDE

During my travels I spent much time in India applying for permission to photograph the Himalayan region. Four years convinced me it was useless; I could not climb any mountain and was probably lucky to have entered the Indian protectorate of Sikkim. Government permission was not needed for Darjeeling and vicinity. The Garhwal Himalayas were off limits; persistent requests to photograph Nanda Devi from close up were all refused.

The Indian government finally allowed me to travel near Manali and Chamba in Himachal Pradesh, returning via Deo Tibba, Indrasan, Mulkila, and Rhotang Pass. The permit from the Indian Mountaineering Foundation of the Defense Ministry was specific: no photographing of military installations; further restrictions could be attached by local commanders; all negatives would be censored. I was overjoyed to receive travel authorization, though I valued its significance too highly. With food, fuel, and equipment for the journey I set off for Manali, my first challenge. The area commander refused me entrance, saying that my warrant was not from the National Defense Ministry. The telephone was for local calls only; I had to drive back to the Ministry in New Delhi and return to Manali with their authorization, impressed with the ineffectiveness of Indian authority. The commander at Manali applied the second of the permit's prohibitions, making my permit worthless. A new permit was issued by the commander: I could walk toward the mountains a few kilometers to a village outside Manali. (Ordinary tourists could travel to Khoksar Pass, twenty kilometers beyond that village.) Two years of trouble were thus rewarded.

THE ROAD TO NANGA PARBAT   (see map, page 22)

Permission from Pakistan authorities to explore Pakistan-controlled Kashmir was not easy. Pakistan was under strict surveillance; one could not enter any government building unless accompanied by a member of one's embassy. For two months I traveled between the Japanese Embassy and the Pakistan government offices, between Rawalpindi in Pakistan and Islamabad in Kashmir.

We entered the mountains in the improbable area of the Astor region. From here we took the path leading to the Lama area and finally to the Lake of Lama, at the end of Sachen Glacier. The days we spent camping by this beautiful lake were relaxing; distant snow-covered mountains loomed over a thick forest. We turned back to Gilgit and went up Rakhiot Glacier. The region is just south of the Indus River but not a tree or blade of grass is to be seen. A deep valley cuts through the desert, carved by the murky water of the Indus, and the spirit of the people seems to reflect the calamitous area. Hunza porters are normally hired, but we could not enter the Hunza area and had to use porters in the Tato area. Expeditions in this region have been plagued by Tato natives, and they made my journey to Nanga Parbat the most trying of my four years in the Himalayas. Once beyond Tato we could not readily turn back to Gilgit. The porters took advantage of the situation and made unreasonable demands: daily strikes for more pay, and walks of only three hours a day before setting their loads down at campsites of their choosing. They worked as porters solely to pilfer, and being armed, could not be admonished. The endless sabotage, strikes, and thefts were very taxing.

The scenery, however, was unbelievably beautiful. Märchen Wiese, the "Wonderland Pasture," a field above Rakhiot Glacier, resembled a well-manicured lawn (Plate 18). A stream rippled by, birds sang in the nearby forests, and the north face of Nanga Parbat stood proudly against the deep blue sky. This was one of the few amiable places in the Himalayas.

Nanga Parbat means "naked mountain" in Sanskrit. Germany sent seven expeditions between 1932 and 1953, and thirty alpinists died before the mountain was successfully scaled. On top of the moraine along Rakhiot Glacier I found the grave of a German climber named Drexel, who died of pneumonia in 1934, the year before I was born. The cross on the grave was in perfect condition and the gravestone well preserved. I laid a bouquet of wild flowers on the grave.

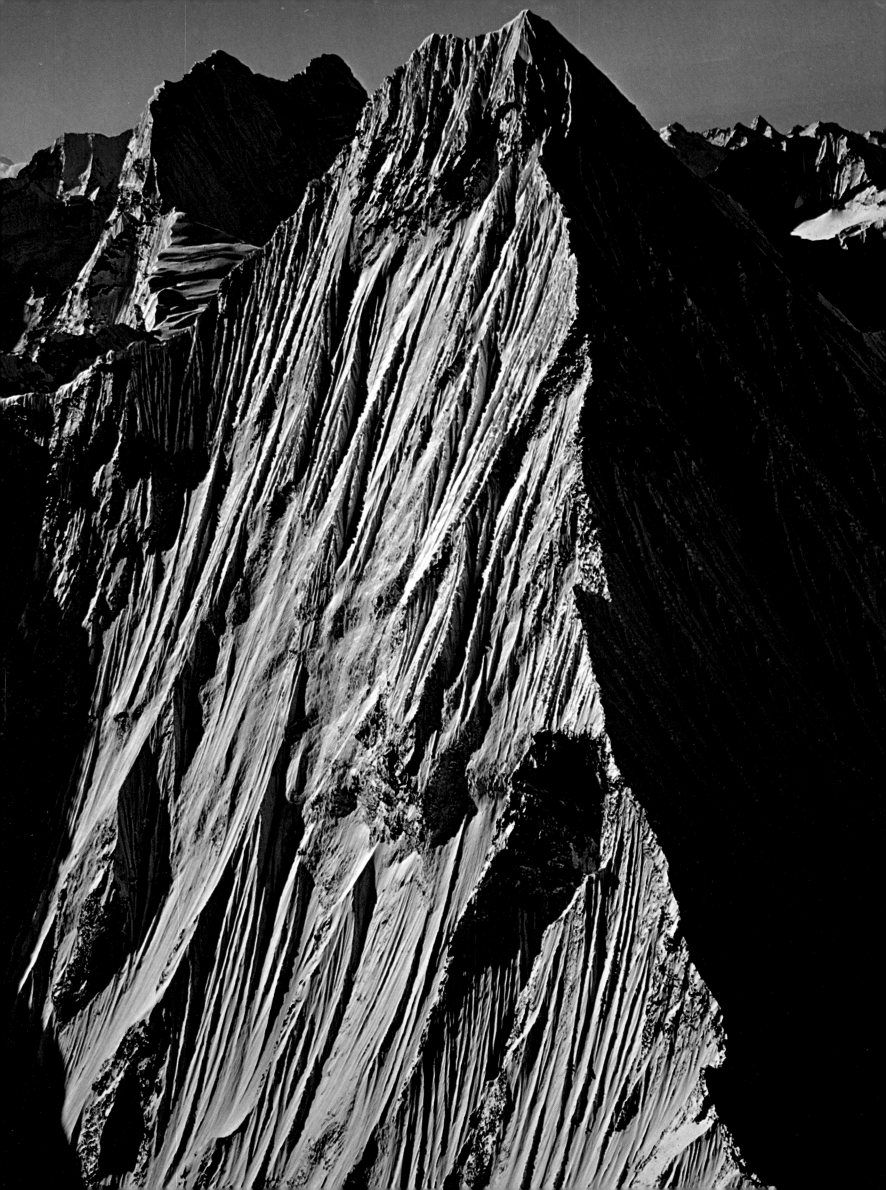

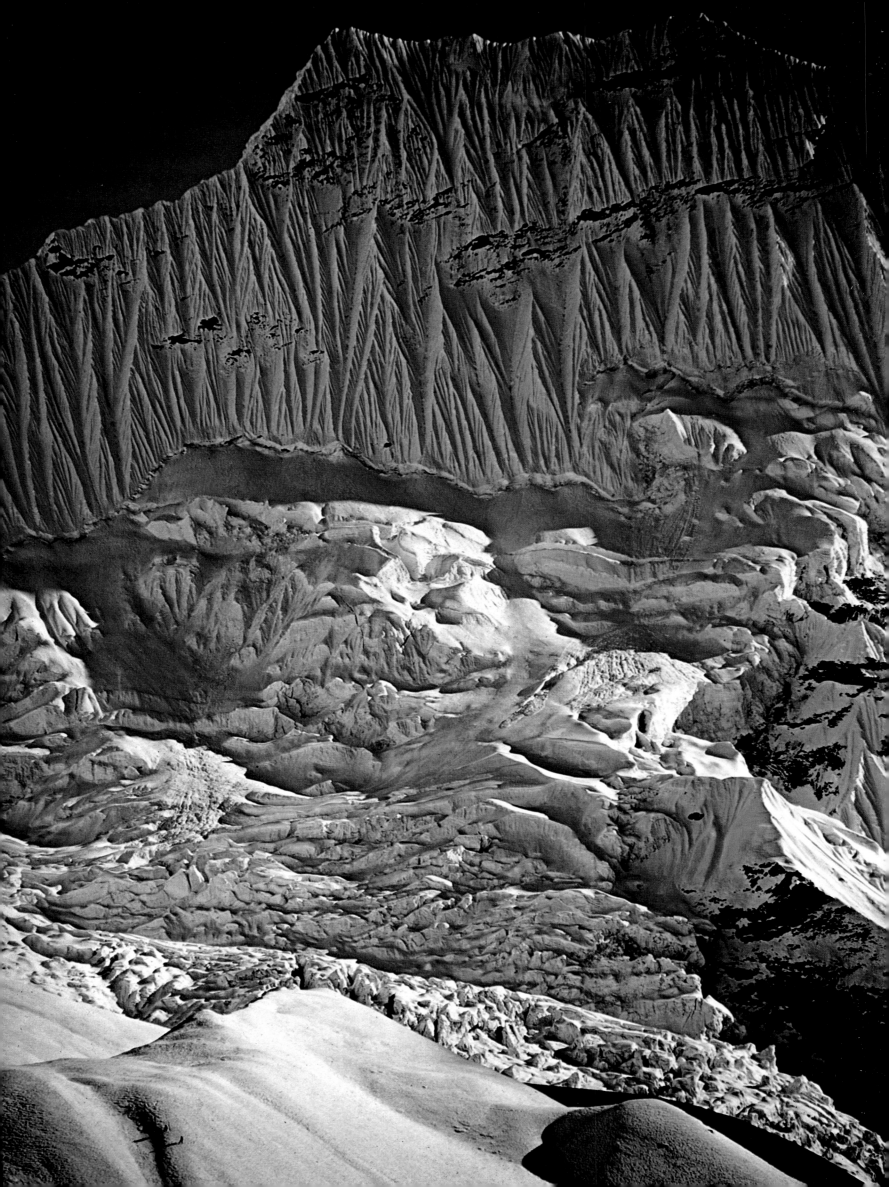

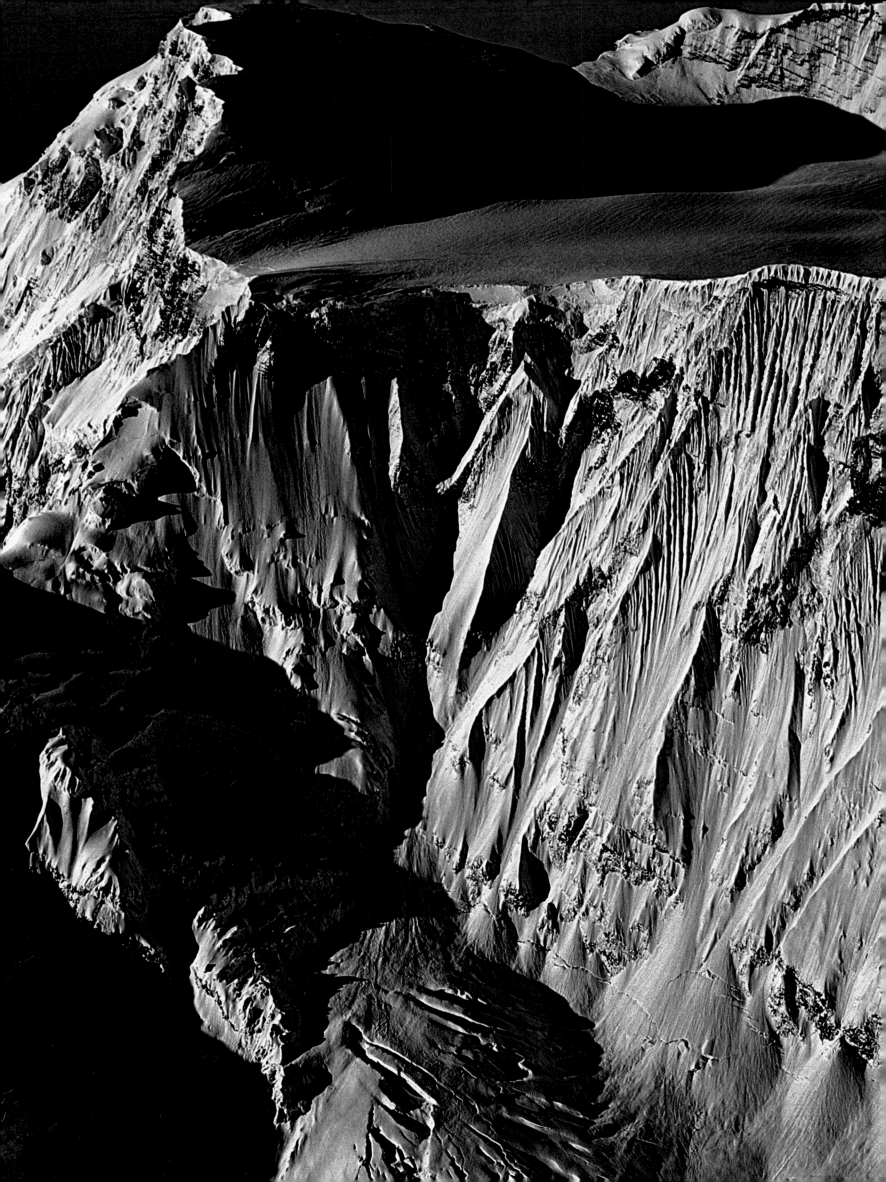

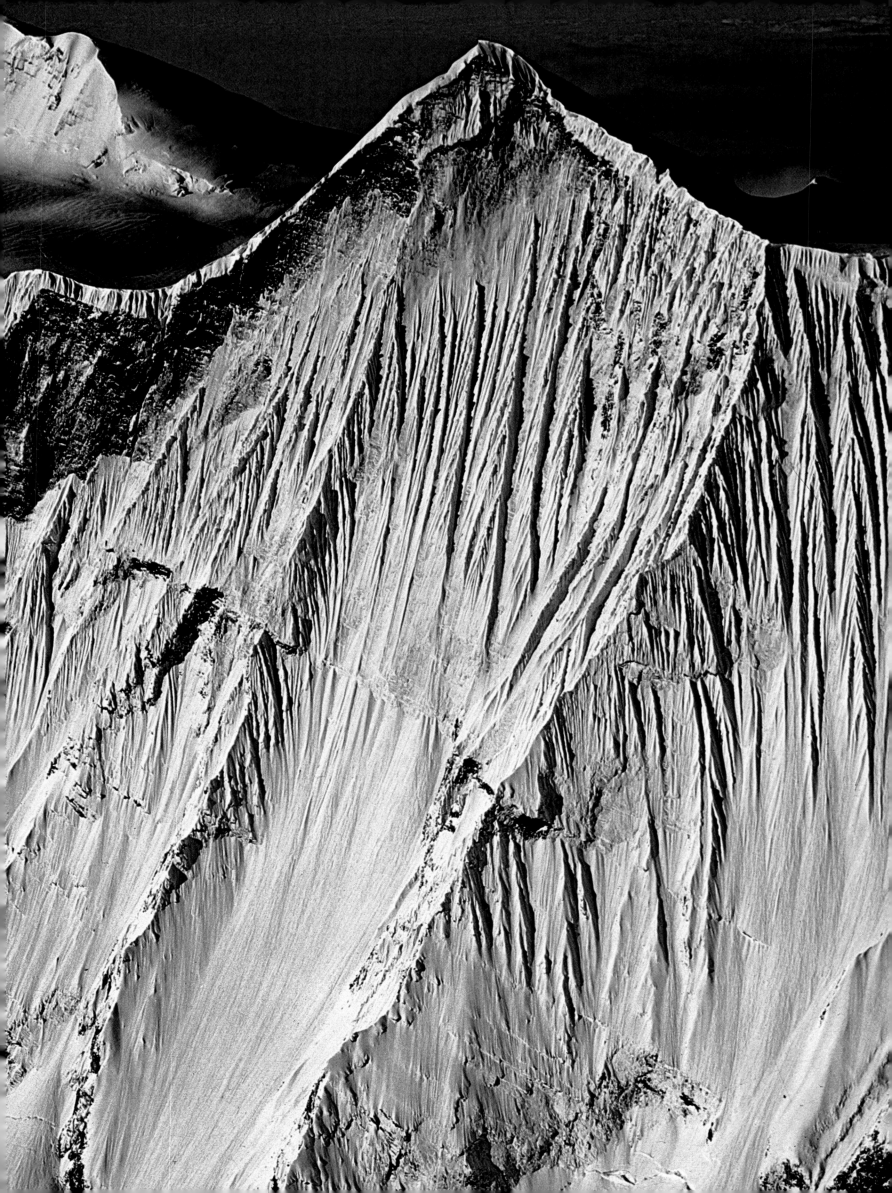

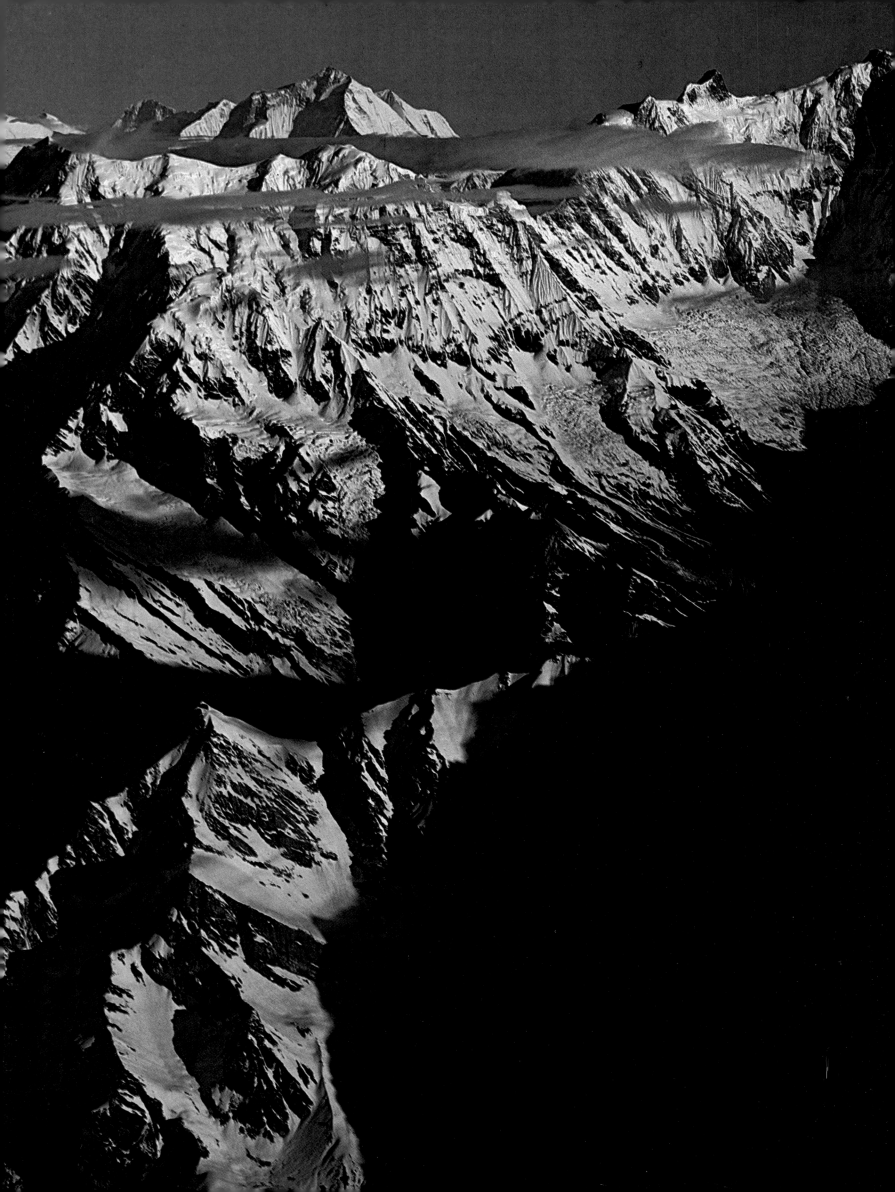

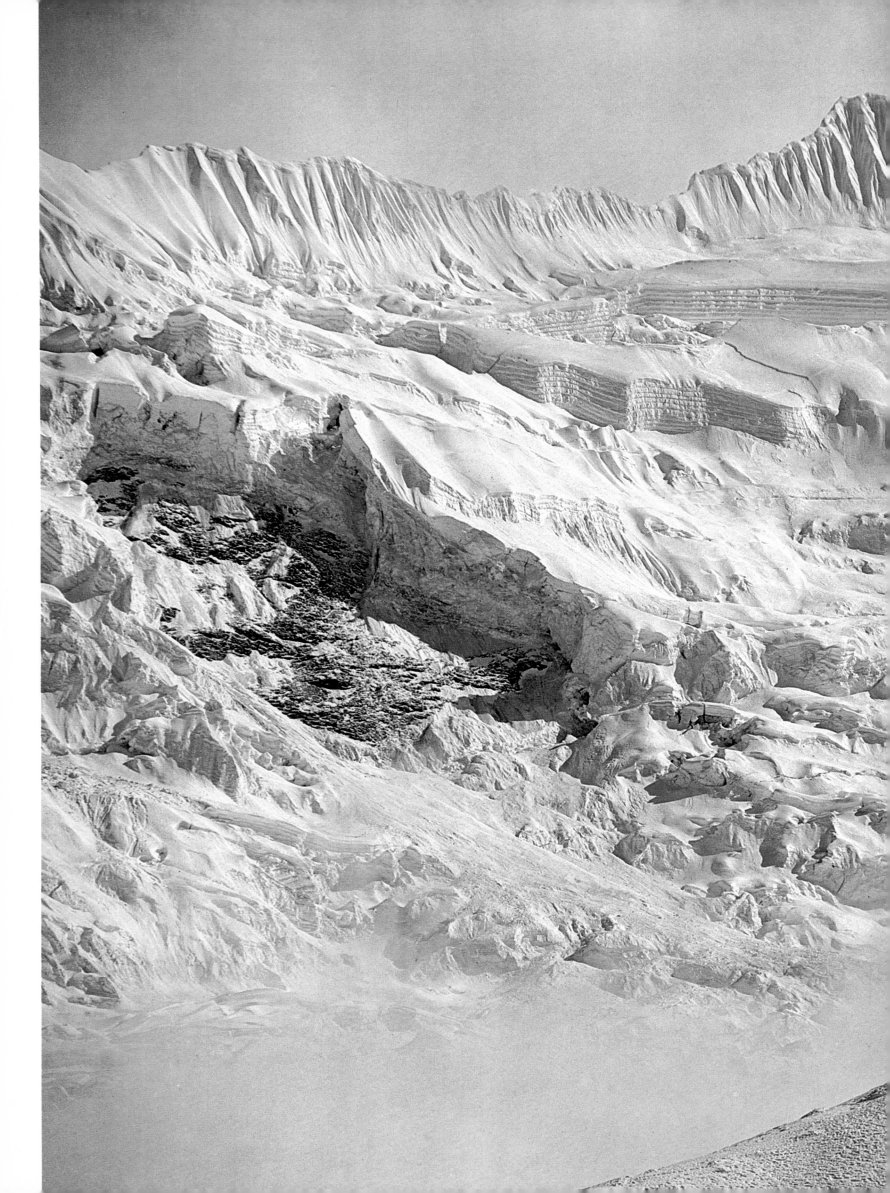

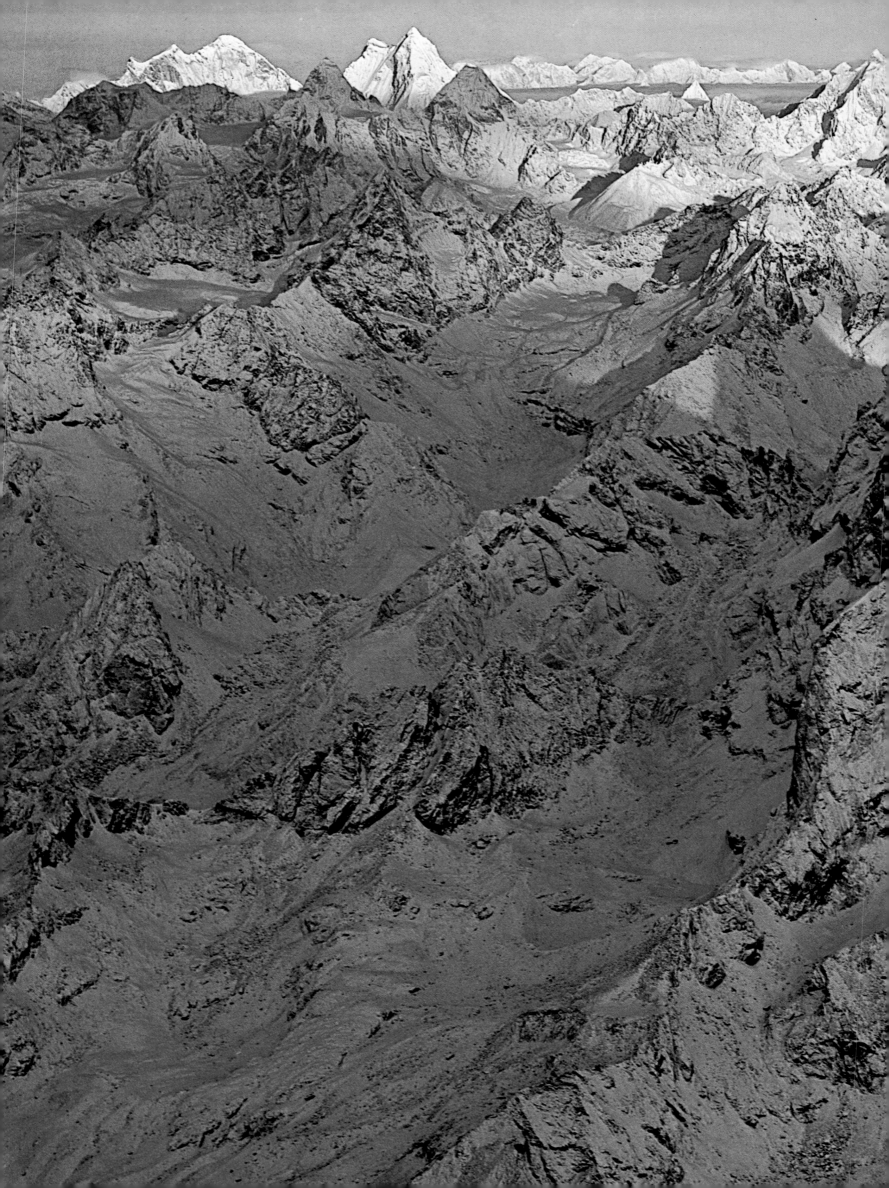

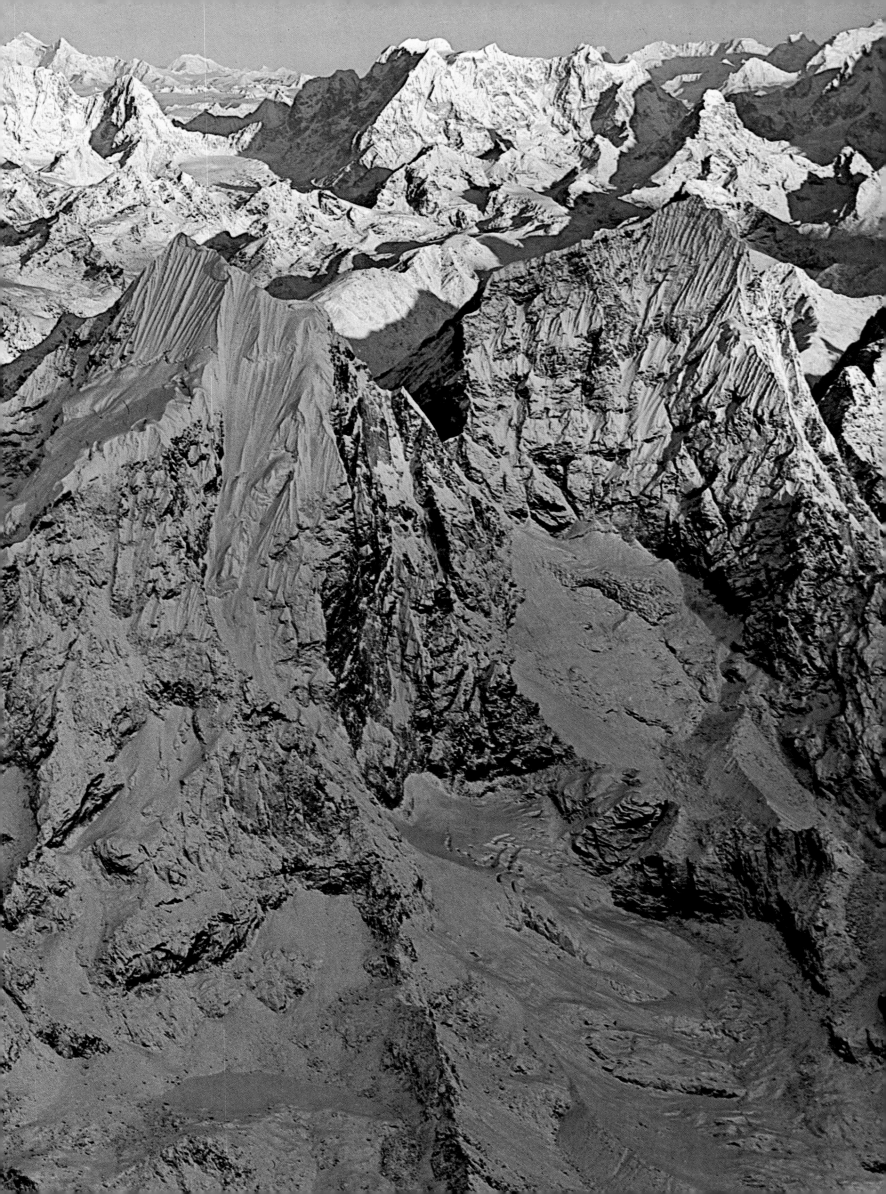

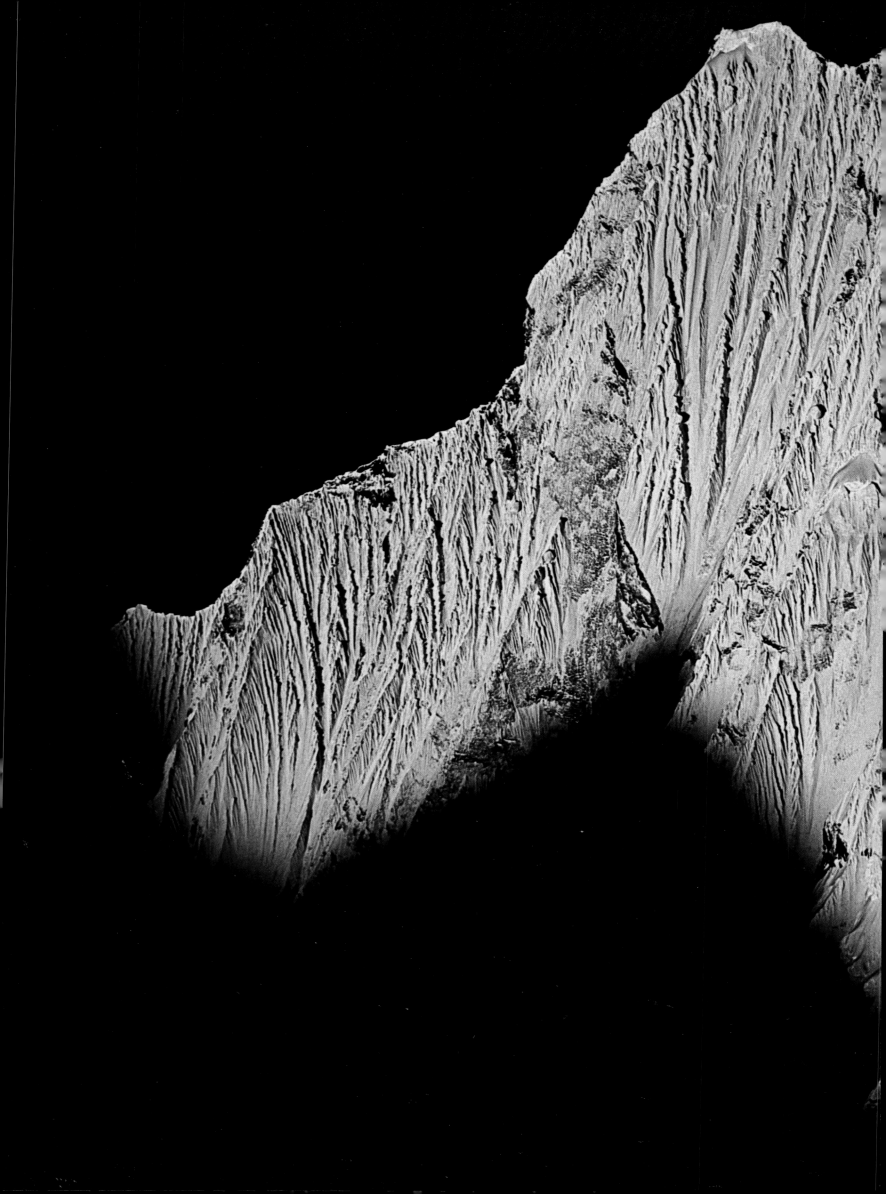

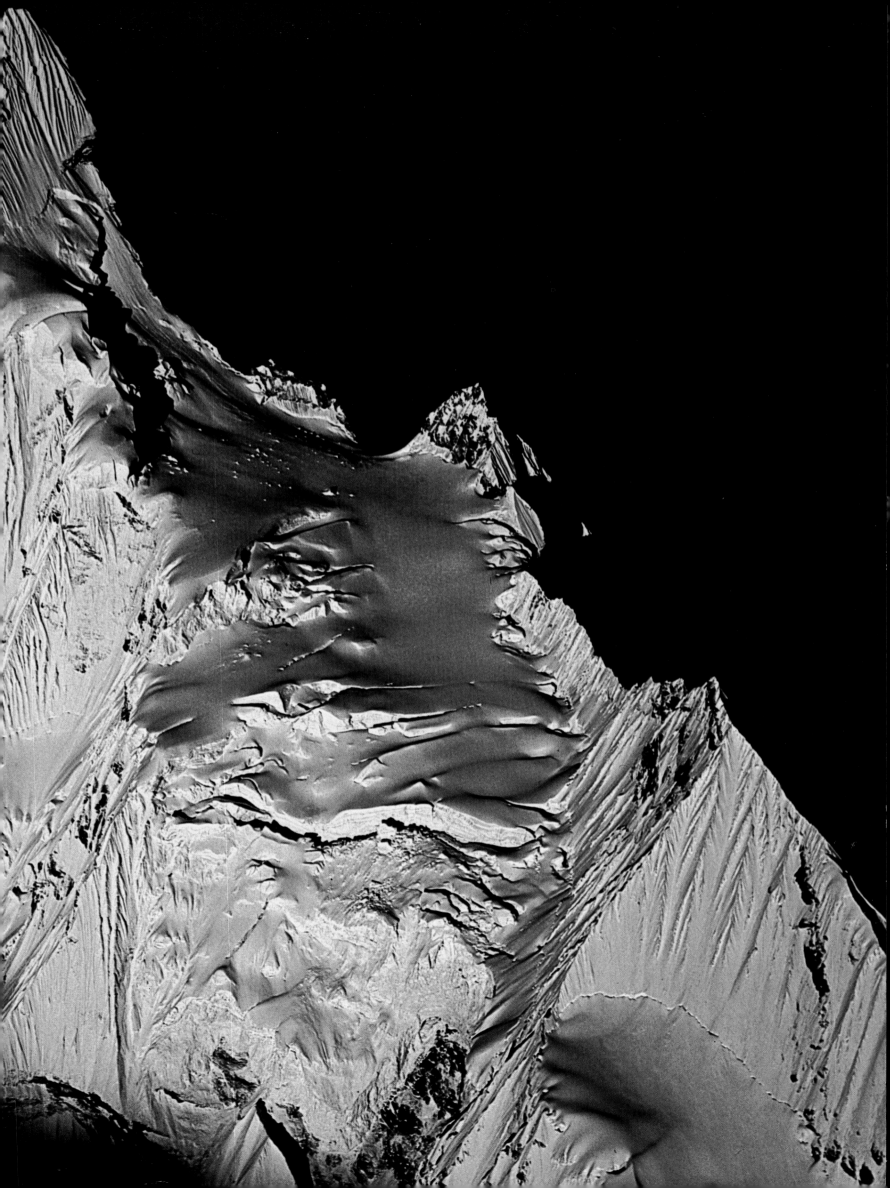

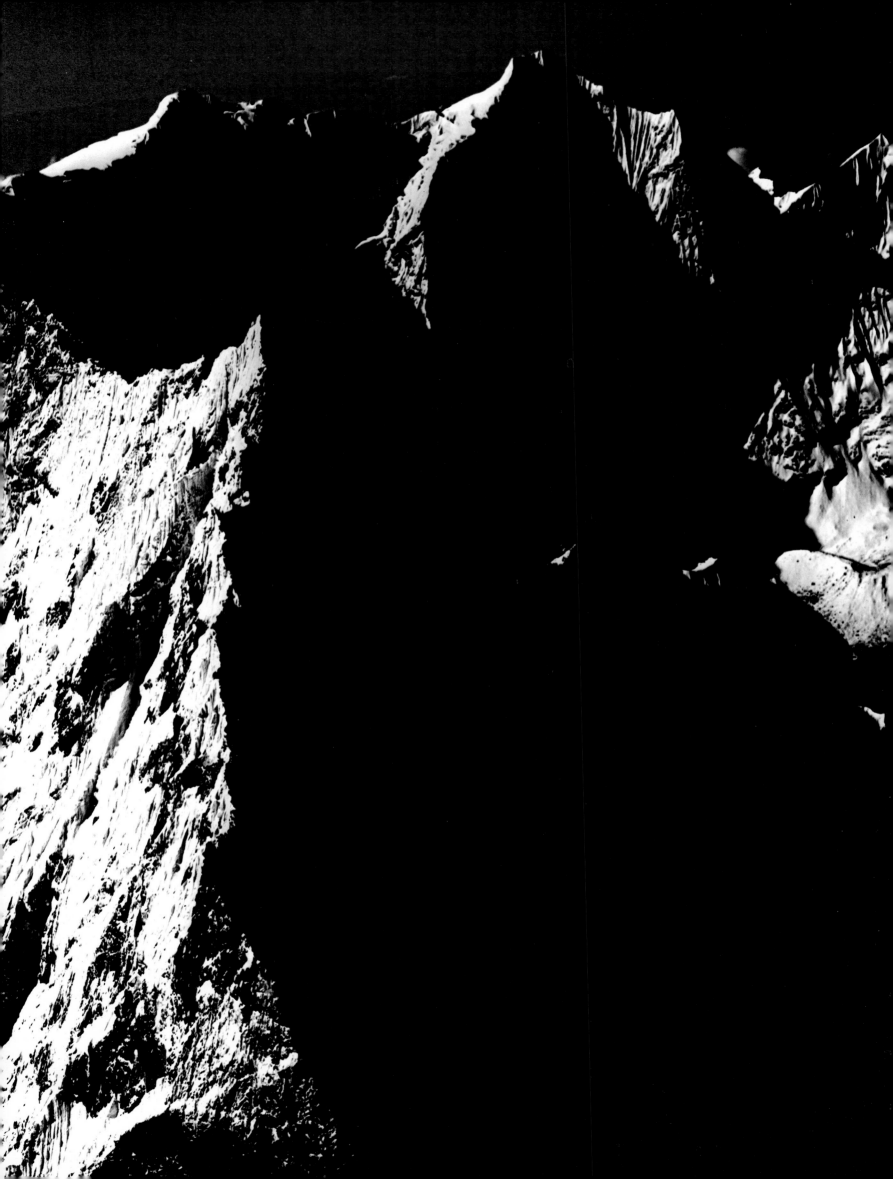

Notes on the Photographs

1. UNNAMED PEAK NORTH OF LUKULA

Lukula airport was one of the air bases for my expedition. When I was told that a small strip on a high plateau was Lukula, our landing place, a chill ran down my spine. The high mountains can create treacherous masses of clear air turbulence; if a plane enters one of these pockets it is luck, as much as the pilot, that guides the plane into calm air and safety. The photograph shows an unnamed peak near Thamserku, north of the landing strip.

2. DHAULAGIRI

Storms of sand and snow battered us daily on our trek along the Kali Gandaki, "Black River." Once we had to stop for two days waiting for the weather to improve. When it cleared I photographed Dhaulagiri, 8,167 meters, with a telescopic lens. In the foreground is Eastern Glacier; the sharp rise on the left is not a peak but a slope. I took air photographs of these mountains, but to me the best view is from the ground at this angle.

3. CHUKHUNG GLACIER

This photography was taken by a member of the party who searched for the *yeti*, the Abominable Snowman. When the mist cleared, the camp was still full of talk about it but we sought it in vain. The sherpa erpa said he had seen the Snowman run across the glacier at mid-slope, which seemed not at all improbable; days are monotonous in the Himalayas and this sort of excitement can be a welcome change.

4. MACHAPUCHARE AT DAWN

The night sky had been clear, not one cloud to dim the overwhelming brilliance of the stars. But when daylight peeked over the horizon, clouds formed gradually. Making a turn above Lamjung Himal, we flew up to 5,500 meters and I shot the southeast face of Machapuchare. The sun's rays created a welcome but unexpected effect, bathing part of the mountain with unnatural color. By flying too low and photographing too close, the mountain is rather misshapen.

5. NORTH SIDE OF LAMJUNG HIMAL

Lamjung Himal, 6,931 meters high, photographed from 7,000 meters. When viewed from the south, as from Pokhara, one sees only one peak; from the north two gently sloping peaks are seen. The triangle-shaped mountain on the right, framed by a ridge, is merely part of one slope. All of these photographs of the Tibetan side of the Annapurna Himal are probably the first ever published.

6. ANNAPURNA I

The higher of Annapurna's two peaks, 8,091 meters, viewed from 7,300 meters. The mountain in the foreground is Machapuchare, 6,993 meters, vaguely resembling a volcano as clouds blow off its peak into the northern sky. Dhaulagiri I, 8,167 meters, is in the far left background; the peak in front of it is Annapurna South, 7,219 meters. Although this mountain looks enormous from the ground, from above it is like a hill among the surrounding giants.

7. AMA DABLAM WITH MOON

As I photographed this beautiful mountain, 6,856 meters high, from Thyangboche Monastery after sunset, I realized that the eastern sky above the mountain was unusually bright, and then the moon appeared. The disks overlap in this picture because a cloud hid the moon for 10 seconds of the 3-minute time exposure. From the monastery, the largest in the area, the view is particularly magnificent.

8. MAKALU
Photographed from 7,700 meters. As our plane approached Makalu, 8,475 meters high, we ran into a powerful flow of air from the north, possibly the jet stream. Our twin-engine Otter was shaken violently; I could barely hold on, let alone take pictures. The turbulence kept us from flying near the mountain walls that day. The peak rising above all others on the left is Everest; to its left is Lhotse. I took this photograph about 5 A.M., after sunrise.

9. UNNAMED PEAK ON HIMALAYA FLUTE
We left our Chukhung camp to photograph the part of Chukhung Glacier that lies beyond Imja Glacier; this photograph was made from Chukhung Glacier. Soon after we had made camp at Chukhung a sherpa reported that he had seen the *yeti,* the Abominable Snowman, running over the glacier. The whole camp became excited and we formed a search party (foreground? ed.). The camp lay in thick fog and the *yeti* might emerge at any time. We were in suspense for days.

10. MOON OVER MACHAPUCHARE
Machapuchare viewed from Gorapani Pass. *Gora* means "horse" and *pani* "water." Countless travelers and caravans have stopped here to water their horses, for the pass is on the main route between Pokhara and Tibet. From here to either Modi Khola or Miristi Khola, the entrances to the pass, takes an entire day's journey.

11. LHOTSE
The view from Chukhung Glacier is one of the most splendid in the Himalayas; the ice towers are like frozen suits of armor. Here Lhotse, 8,501 meters, stands in the center, about to be wrapped in darkness. The peak on the left is Nuptse, 7,879 meters. One never wearies of the majesty of this area. It is especially impressive when, as the sun sets, the first stars appear.

12. MT. EVEREST
The earth's tallest peak, Everest rises 8,848 meters high. Lhotse, 8,501 meters, is far right of Everest; between them stands the rugged hulk of 7,879-meter Nuptse. From a hill behind our Gokyo camp on the western bank of Ngojumba Glacier I spent all day photographing Everest from various angles. At sunset she revealed her splendor, her southern face flamed scarlet by the setting sun. I took this picture as New Year's Day, 1969, was relinquishing its light.

13. MACHAPUCHARE IN CLOUDS
I hiked west from Pokhara for a day to get a partial view of the western wall and summit of Machapuchare. From the path on the Nadara ridge I photographed the mountain at evening time; I had another shot from there of Annapurna's peak protruding from the clouds. It was hard to decide which to include in this volume, but I finally chose this view of Machapuchare. Its ridge is sharply defined and the striped pattern of the red clouds gives an interesting photographic effect.

14. ANNAPURNA HIMAL AT SUNSET
We were flying at about 7,300 meters on the way back from photographing Manaslu's three peaks when I took this shot of Annapurna South, the peak to the left of the sun. Annapurna I is in the clouds under the sun; Machapuchare is in the foreground, its peak reflecting the setting rays. These mountains form a fairly sharp line. Pokhara is deep in the valley to the left; darkness was creeping over it as we flew back.

15. HIMALAYA RANGE
This photograph looking northwest at 7,000 meters shows Taweche (6,543 meters) in the center foreground and Cholatse (6,440 meters) to the right. Gaurisankar (7,150 meters) is in the far left background, with Menlungtse's two peaks (7,181 meters) at its right. Cut off at far right is an unnamed peak (7,352 meters); famous Cho Oyu, not visible, is further right. Mountains piercing the clouds and those beyond are in Tibet.

16. EASTERN WALL OF MACHAPUCHARE
This photograph makes one think at once of the Matterhorn in the Alps. The two mountains so strongly resemble each other that they are hard to tell apart. In this volume I have photographs of Machapuchare from east, west, and south; the eastern wall offers the best views. We circled at 7,000 meters until the shadows gave me this picture.

17. PANORAMA OF KATHMANDU
Kathmandu, capital of Nepal, seen toward the northeast from near the summit of Chandra Gil, 2,831 meters high. It is only during November and December that the city and the surrounding Himalayas can be seen this clearly. At the left is Shisha Pangma (Gosainthan); Ganesh Himal and Annapurna Himal lie further left. Far to the right the mountains around Everest are clearly visible.

18. MÄRCHEN WIESE
The "Wonderland Pasture" north of Rakhiot Glacier was given this name by the German expedition that climbed Nanga Parbat in 1932. The spot is certainly a pleasant one and the northern face of the mountain spectacular. Alas, the thievery of the Tato porters, and their lazy, opportunistic behavior, spoiled our trip.

19. CHILDREN AT GHANSA
Ghansa is a day's hike beyond Tatopani, northwest from Pokhara. On the village outskirts an azure lake makes camping quite pleasant. North from there sand storms whip across Kali Gandaki Glacier. These children were at a rest house where we stopped near Ghansa. The infants' eyes are all strongly penciled. I suppose these children are Nepal Hindu; it is difficult to tell apart the sixteen different ethnic groups in Nepal.

20. WOMAN AT TATOPANI
I made a one-day excursion to Tatopani, going through Gorapani Pass via Sikha. Travel was not tiring, since no climbing was involved. Towering Dhaulagiri was in breathtaking contrast to the gradually descending slope we crossed. At the bottom is Kali Gandaki River; Tatopani ("hot water") refers to two hot springs on the river banks. I took this photograph there; from the young woman's makeup and dress I think she is Nepal Hindu, not sherpa or Bhotiya.

21. MUSICIAN
Itinerant singers like the man in this photograph might be called strolling musicians or minstrels—no single term fits them. They wait at the places where caravans stop. The compensation for singing four or five songs is 50 piasas, about a nickel. This photograph, taken in Siswa, shows a singer with a fish he has received in payment. He is happy because fish is rare in Nepal. His voice was delicate and melancholy.

22. AMA DABLAM AND THYANGBOCHE MONASTERY
The largest lamasery in Thyangboche district, this monastery is erected on a huge plateau above Imja Glacier and offers a panoramic view of the entire region. Nearby, Ama Dablam stands at 6,856 meters. I photographed the area from the air, but this view from the ground was far better. The contrast of the splendid white mountain and brick-colored monastery (right foreground) makes a lasting impression on the viewer.

23. MOUNTAINS AROUND GANESH HIMAL
Photographed from the air toward the north. Ganesh Himal, 7,406 meters high, is at the left on the Tibet-Nepal border. Wind-blown clouds mark a 7,130-meter unnamed peak in the center. (I checked with many people to see if this figure is correct, but got no definite answer.) Another high mountain is Pabil Peak on the right, 7,102 meters.

24. WALL OF THAMSERKU
From the ground Thamserku's sculptured outline is very beautiful. I had hoped to take a good photograph from the air, and tried a close-up directly from the front; at whatever angle or altitude, the view was far less fine than I had expected. The mountain's highest point is 6,608 meters; the sharp peak of Thamserku seen from the ground is at bottom right, hidden in the shadow of the mountain's full height.

25. NANGA PARBAT FROM TALICHI
The finest view of Nanga Parbat from the road following the Indus River is from the area near Talichi village, some twenty buildings around an oasis in the grey-colored desert. In summer fierce sand storms strike every evening, and temperatures during the day rise to 105° F. The turbid Indus flows dark brown through this region.

SIKKIM HIMALAYAS

HINDU KUSH

The Sikkim Himalayas

Most of the Himalayan ranges extend from east to west, formed from the north-south squeeze between the land masses of Central Asia and India. Only the Sikkim Himalayas, on the Sikkim–Nepal border, run north to south. In this range are the earth's third highest peak, Kangchenjunga (8,598 meters), and thirteen mountains over 7,000 meters: particularly famous are Jannu in Nepal and Siniolchu in Sikkim. Jannu, the most awesome high peak in the whole Himalaya chain, is called ''The Sleeping Lion,'' ''The Sphinx,'' ''The Monster,'' and other names that hint at its reputation among alpinists. It competes with Kangchenjunga in its breathtaking appearance and its popularity, but knowledge about it is scant, since Nepal has never readily let foreigners in. Nepal relaxed its restrictions in 1949, but reinstated its isolationist policy in 1963. Few foreigners enter the country today, and those who do usually have restricted movement. Ours was the only group ever to travel throughout the Sikkim Himalayas. For a complete view of the range, the area must be explored from the Sikkim side and from Nepal. I began on the Sikkim side.

Mountains in this range were first scaled from Sikkim in the late nineteenth century. The British had great interest in the Himalayas, and sent out many expeditions. From Darjeeling, the starting point for mountain assaults in the region, one can view the entire Sikkim Himalayas; at 2,000 meters above sea level, the city once provided the British a cool retreat from the summer heat of India, the closest mountains only 70 kilometers away. Now the Indian population has increased, and Darjeeling contrasts with the splendor of its surroundings. To appreciate the grandeur of the Sikkim Himalayas one must stand on Tiger Hill, eleven kilometers southeast of Darjeeling (Plate 35). Most photographs of the majestic Sikkim Himalayas have been taken from there, and our conception of the entire Himalayan complex has been influenced by these views.

ENTRY INTO SIKKIM

I never expected permission to photograph the mountains of Sikkim and Bhutan, but I heard that I might enter those countries just after hearing that my requests to enter the Indian mountains had been denied. Mr. P. N. Mennon, General Director of the Northern Territorial Bureau of the Indian Ministry of Foreign Affairs, suggested the Sikkim alternative; I had known him three years, since requesting admission to the Garhwal Himalayas and the Indian side of the Punjab Himalayas. My disappointment at not being able to photograph the Garhwal and Punjab Himalayas was great, but I decided to apply for travel to Sikkim. Mennon got me the permit the next day. He suggested that I visit Bhutan as well, but he left his position two weeks before I was scheduled to receive permission, and the new director was unwilling to issue the interline pass. I had to abandon the plan.

I discussed the situation with my Japanese publishers; our original plan covered all of the Himalaya Range, and we wished to include at least some photographs taken in Bhutan, but if we went to Bhutan for two snapshots, with attendant delays and expenses, and spent $5,500, the total for the book might end up in millions!

Our plans for Bhutan had collapsed, but the trip to Sikkim went smoothly. We flew from New Delhi to Baghdogra, and drove to Darjeeling. Thick clouds hid the mountains for three days; with the eight-day time limit on our stay in Sikkim we had to leave Darjeeling, hoping for a clear view of the mountains on the way back. We drove by jeep to Gangtok, the capital of Sikkim, via Kalimpong, following the stipulations in our permit. Road construction stopped us for hours at a time, and three checkpoints delayed us further. I had heard that Sikkim permissions were usually limited to one day, three days at the most; one day spent in reaching Gangtok means another day to drive back; such restrictions effectively prevent visitors from seeing much of the country. But my friend Mennon had obtained permission for us for eight days, and for us to travel about eighty kilometers north of Gangtok. We had not dared hope to enter this more mountainous region; with only five days left, I had not yet reached the northern limit of my journey. We drove along the highway connecting India and Sikkim. At night Indian army trucks passed by and guns were hauled up the highway; Natu La, the pass where Indian and Chinese armies clash occasionally, is only eight kilometers northeast of Gangtok. The unpaved road was wide and well constructed. Kalimpong, Gangtok, Natu La, then around the foot of Mt. Chomolhari in Bhutan, and on to Kangmar in Tibet: this was the main route through the mountains until the pass turned into a battlefield.

The close view of the mountains did not yield interesting photographic subjects. Photographs of Kangchenjunga taken from Darjeeling are spectacular, and I had expected that from Gangtok a close-up of the mountains in the Kangchenjunga area would be even better. But the eastern side of Kangchenjunga was remarkably unimpressive; no part of this view even hinted at its splendor. I drove back to Darjeeling to photograph Kangchenjunga from there. The mountain, somewhat flat on top, is more dramatic when partly hidden in clouds than on clear days.

NEPALESE SIDE OF THE SIKKIM HIMALAYAS   (see map, page 25)

The Sikkim trip having produced unsatisfying photographs, I desperately wanted to cover this mighty range with pictures of the Nepalese side, or a view from the top of the mountains. With no hope of receiving permission, I applied for entry into the Nepalese mountains; miraculously, I heard that my party would be the first since the country closed in 1963 to tour the mountains, thanks to the Japanese Embassy and the generosity of Brigadier General Sushil Shumsher J. B. Rana.

I flew from Kathmandu Airport to Biratnagar, then drove as far as Dharan Bazar, where we pitched camp in the Nepalese mountains. I was soon interrupted by Indian soldiers; India had set up a checkpoint and an official demanded an Indian permit, ignoring my guarantee from the Nepalese government. We were in Nepal, but they claimed the area was in India. I explained to the officer who I was, showed them all my credentials, and mentioned the names of Mr. Mennon of the Indian Ministry of Foreign Affairs and Mr. Sarhin, the Secretary General of the National Defense Ministry. They finally let me pass. I later told the incident to the Nepalese Foreign Ministry at Kathmandu but the officers dismissed it with a laugh; yet I often saw Indian officials in Nepalese territory acting like conquerors. Indian checkpoints in Nepal are said to be disappearing, and they should.

Early the next day, January 6, 1970, we began our march; the sherpas were Happa Tenzing, Annu, and Gartzen, and we had fifteen porters. Our party of twenty-one included myself and my assistants Kihara and Tanioka. The walk to Ghunsa, for a close-up view of the mountains, was to take about three weeks; I hastened our march by paying the porters extra to walk until dark every day, reaching Ghunsa in two weeks. We crossed Chunjerma Pass and passed the ruins of Tseram, an old village. On our maps were four villages along our route, but we saw only ruins; nor did we find the ruined monastery or the tombs of Lama monks mentioned in old descriptions of the area.

Twenty days out of Dharan Bazar I took my first photograph of the Nepalese–Sikkim Himalayas, a splendid view of Kangchenjunga towering over Yalung Glacier (Plate 39). The route of the British expedition to the summit was clearly visible; the eastern face of Jannu was also in sight. The top of the glacier is a few thousand meters high, formed of unbelievably white snow and ice; it slides down to meet the Eastern Jannu Glacier. The view was far more spectacular than I had imagined.

In the fall of 1899, the Italian Alpine photographer Vittorio Sella and the English climber Douglas Freshfield, who later became the head of the British Alpine Society, journeyed around Kangchenjunga, an important event in the history of photography. They crossed Johnsan Pass to enter Nepal, but the country was closed to foreigners and they were chased out when found by a Nepalese soldier at Kangbacheng Village. On their way back to Sikkim they crossed Chunjerma Pass, and photographed the view of Jannu that makes the Italian photographer still famous in photography circles. Standing where Sella stood over seventy years ago, facing the same mountain, I reflected on his emotions (Plates 27, 47).

It took us two days to walk from Ghunsa to Tseram through snowstorms, battered by violent winds. My ears were frost-bitten. The second day was worse because two porters deserted, their loads then divided among a sherpa and my assistants. Since the area has never been fully surveyed it is difficult to obtain accurate charts. I had a map from Japan, and I had purchased one in India. We had been through five passes, three of them marked on one map and four on the other; Chunjerma Pass had to be one of these. But both maps were wrong, and I wasted time finding the real Chunjerma Pass: this later brought unexpected danger to the entire party.

The fifth pass, that closest to Tseram, was far from where the historical photograph was taken, so we headed back to the third pass. When I arrived Tanioka, who had gone ahead, told me he had seen Jannu, though all the mountains were now in clouds. Hoping Tanioka was right, I decided to camp until the clouds cleared, though the weather was worsening. We pitched our tents in the snow-and-ice-covered pass, a difficult task at 5,000 meters because of the strong winds. Our thermometer registered no lower than −20°C., but the temperature was well below −30°C. While we ate, a sherpa burst in to tell us that Jannu was right above our heads. Everybody dashed out; the red glow of the sky, dotted with moving clouds, was the backdrop for the mountain I had dreamed of. I felt consumed by the majestic, overwhelming massiveness of the mountain. I spent three days in this icy, stormy pass, photographing the ever-changing Jannu every minute I could (Plates 32, 33).

In Ghunsa we rested and replenished our supplies, then followed the Ghunsa River north to Pang Pema, where we stayed three days. On the way back to Kangbacheng, I detoured to the top of Ramtang Glacier and stopped by Jannu Glacier

(Plate 26). Although it was the dry season, it started to snow; in three years I had never encountered such weather in the Himalayas, and we were unprepared for snow. We were bogged down for a week.

We had planned to return to Ghunsa Village in two days, and food now became a serious problem. Our supplies ran out in four days, except for emergency rations; on the eighth day we decided to try for Ghunsa. Split into three groups, we left at thirty-minute intervals, that one group might survive if a snowslide struck. Below Kangbacheng we had to cross a steep expanse two or three kilometers long, the most dangerous part of our escape plan; we saw snow roar down across the area we must traverse in this suicidal attempt, but we could not stay where we were.

I was in the third group and saw the others far ahead, running, slipping, and stumbling through the snow. They advanced slowly. The first group was breaking new snow, so the second caught up with them in the middle of the steep expanse. Scars of massive snowslides were visible above and below, and another might crash down while we watched. I had to look away.

I have often met danger and do not myself fear death, but in my Himalaya travels I took every precaution for the lives of the sherpas and my assistants. All of our party survived without serious injuries; in my three years in the Himalayas I was fortunate that no one was killed in any party I led. My experiences made me believe in the existence of some higher power, awesome and difficult to describe.

The Hindu Kush Range

The Hindu Kush mountain range extends southwest, from the southern extreme of the Pamir Plateau to the easternmost point at longitude 68° east. Most of the high peaks in the range are along the Pakistan–Afghanistan border and its surrounding area, where the Hindu Kush mountains mentioned here are located. We must be specific, for some geographers consider the Hindu Kush range to be 1,200 kilometers long, including the mountains of Koh-i-Baba and Safed Koh and extending the range to Iran's border: the Himalayas themselves would then have a total length of 4,000 kilometers. But the mountains west of longitude 68° east are only 2,000 to 4,000 meters high; most Himalaya mountains are 6,000 to 7,000 meters high, and such low ''mountains'' do not seem to belong in the range. In this book the entire Himalayan Range is some 3,000 kilometers long, from the eastern edge of the Assam Himalayas at longitude 96° east to the western edge of the Hindu Kush at longitude 68° east.

Pakistan's Tirich Mir, 7,706 meters above sea level, is the highest peak of the Hindu Kush. Along the Afghanistan border lie beautiful mountains such as Istor-o-Nal (7,403 meters) and Noshaq (7,492 meters). Formerly travelers from Kabul toward the Indus Plain used the passes along this border: the Khyber Pass (1,029 meters), still used today; and Khawak Pass, where the invading armies of Alexander the Great and Tamerlane (Timur) crossed the Himalayas.

PAKISTAN SIDE   (see map, page 25)

The name ''Hindu Kush'' first recalls our travel across torturously hot deserts. Except for a few hours each morning and evening, the desert heat was unbearable—more trying than icy −40°C. weather in the mountains. The mid-day temperature made breathing difficult. We would cool off our heads and soak our feet in any stream of water, but the heat finally made walking impossible; when the blisters broke on the soles of our feet we had to charter donkeys and horses. I shall never forget crossing those fiery sands.

I flew to Chitral to visit Shahsadar Burhranudin Khan, whom I had met several times in Rawalpindi. Chitral was once independent, and Shahsadar, a title similar to ''Lord,'' was its king. During World War II he commanded the Indian national army, organized under Chandra Bose, which fought for Indian independence. His kindness far surpassed ordinary goodwill, and he met my every need. Our caravan, including ten porters and one guide, left Chitral with my assistant and myself riding horses, gifts from Shahsadar. We first went through Siogot, then came to narrow mountain paths and proceeded on foot. We passed Susm and crossed Owir An (4,338 meters) on the third day, crawling up the steep, snowy slope with the sun's reflection adding to our difficulties. I scooped up snow to stuff in my cap, the cold water providing relief as it melted down my face. Our destination was Tirich Glacier. The difficult Owir An is not included in the normal route, but it offers a fine panoramic view for taking pictures. At Kosht we returned to the regular route, crossed Zani An Pass, and entered Tirich Glacier, where I took pictures for a week (Plate 40).

On the way back, we passed by Bandok and descended to Kosht after crossing the Kosht An. The road had disappeared in the snow. Our guide had left us, and my assistant and I were hard pressed to find the way. From Kosht we took the regular route to Maroi by way of Reshun (Plate 42). The path beyond Maroi widens enough for a jeep; in Maroi we found a jeep, thoughtfully sent for us by Shahsadar.

AFGHANISTAN REGION

In 1969, I obtained permission to take aerial photographs of the Afghanistan region of the Hindu Kush Range. I wanted good weather, hoping to catch the mountains covered in new snow, and I went back to Kabul late in October with two assistants. The weather was quite bad; after waiting three weeks we postponed the work until the following year. In late June 1970, I flew to Kabul on the Afghanistan government airline. Permission to photograph the Band-i-Amir area had been a simple matter (Plates 43, 45), but approaching the Russo-Pakistan border by plane was more difficult.

According to the pilot, flying near the border can be a harrowing experience; he refused to make the trip unless the airline had positive guarantees that the Russian and Pakistan governments would not shoot at us. The Afghanistan government wired twice to the air force headquarters of both countries, in Tashkent (U.S.S.R.) and Rawalpindi (Pakistan), respectively, with no answers. As the government was on friendly terms with both Russia and Pakistan, we decided to fly to Kunduz and wait for final confirmation of our request there. My plan was to photograph from the plane just after sunrise. At dinner time that evening our pilot brought word that both countries had agreed, and we all toasted the news. But at the airport before sunrise the radio operator was busily replying to a wireless call. Permission had been revoked: one of the countries, with an abrupt about-face attitude, announced that it would follow international custom and shoot at aircraft invading its national border.

So we flew east for perhaps ten minutes before Noshaq and other high peaks first picked up the morning sun. Forty kilometers from the border the pilot would go no further, and circled south. I photographed the mountains in the central Hindu Kush on our way back to Kabul (Plates 41, 48, 49). Paying there for our chartered flight was not an easy matter; I was charged sixty per cent more than the sum agreed on, and was told I could not leave until I met their demand. Calls were made to government authorities, and men gathered threateningly around me until I paid the additional amount.

The Himalayas are indeed beautiful; no place on earth can match their splendid scenery. Unfortunately, the attitudes of some people living there are in contrast with this dazzling beauty, and unpleasant experiences spoil my recollections of an otherwise enjoyable stay.

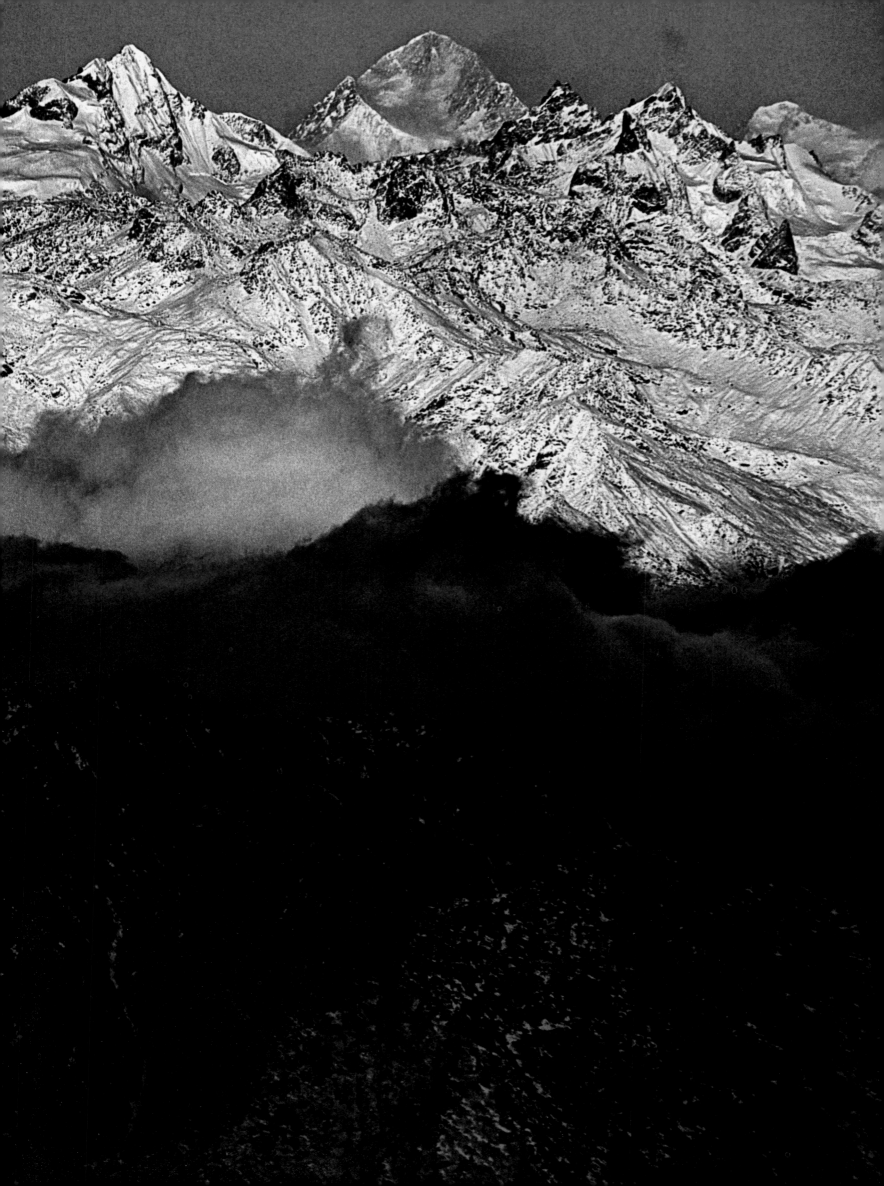

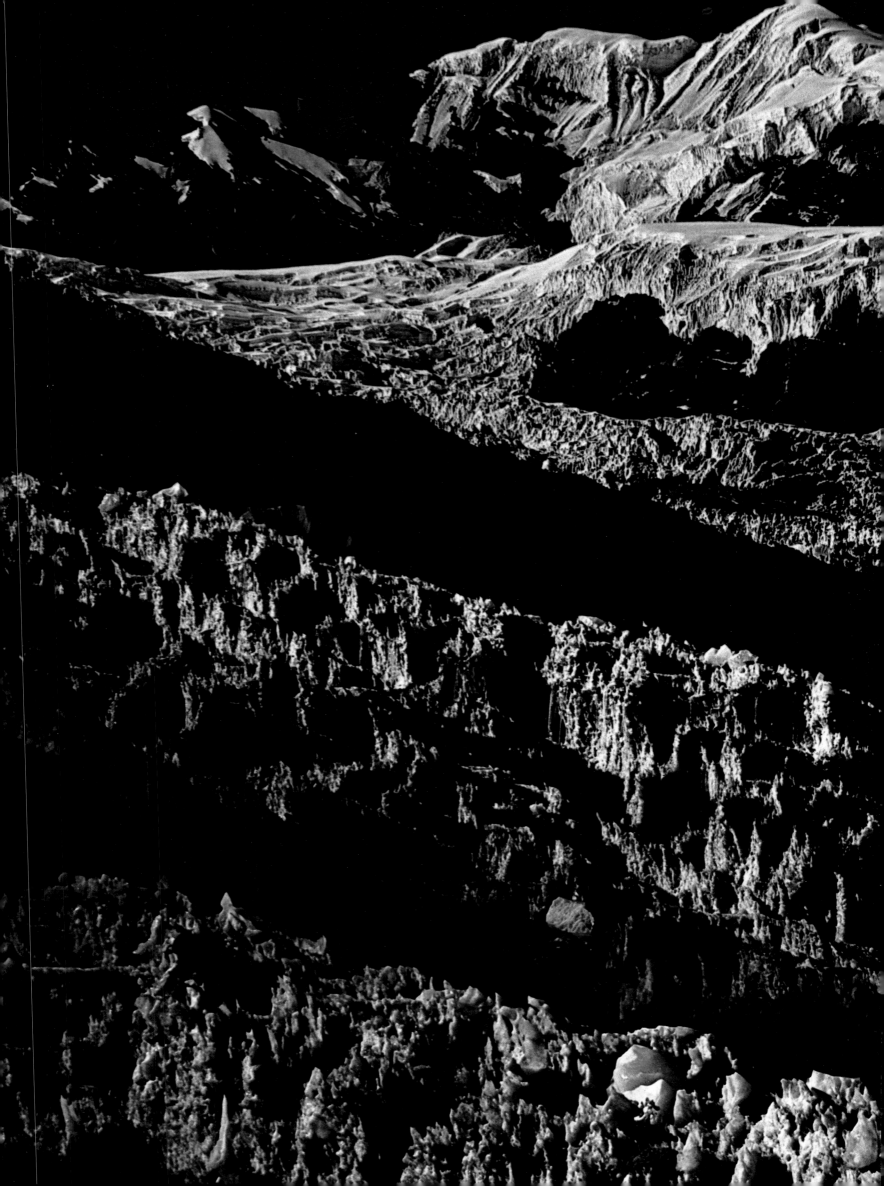

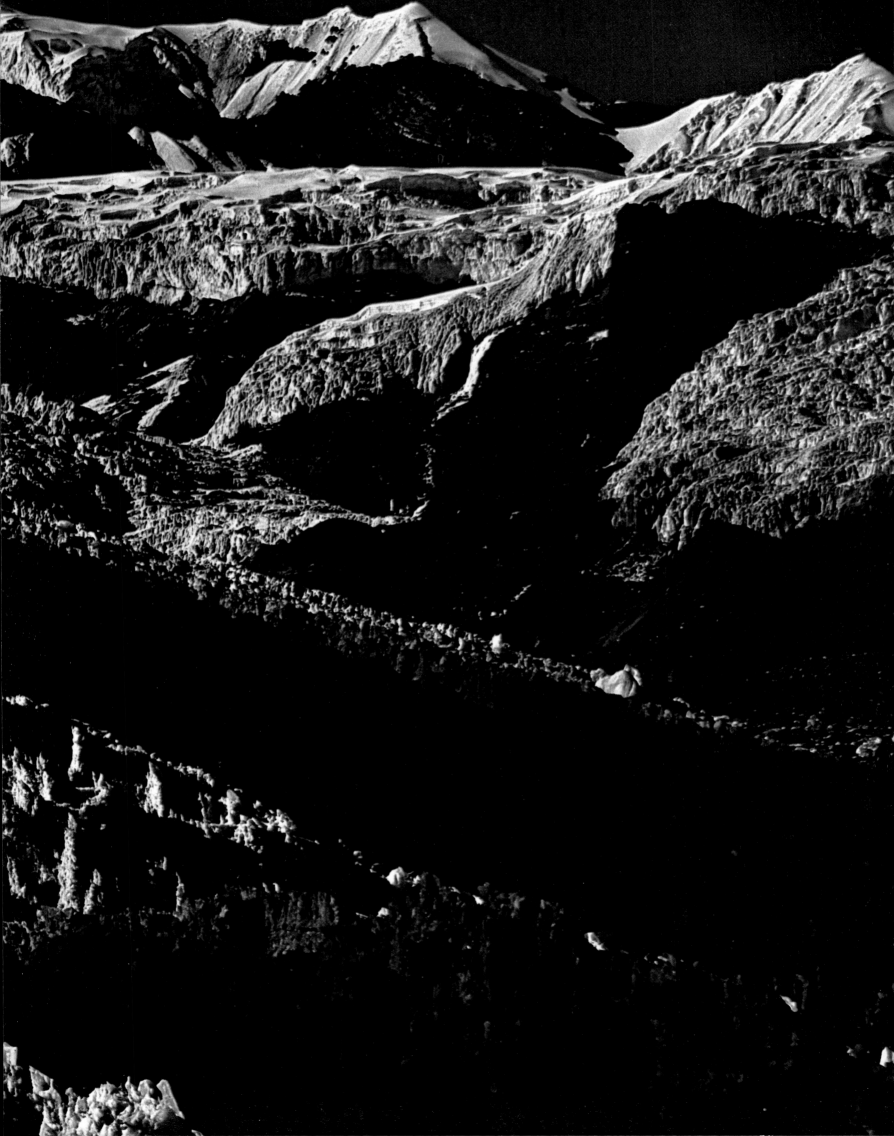

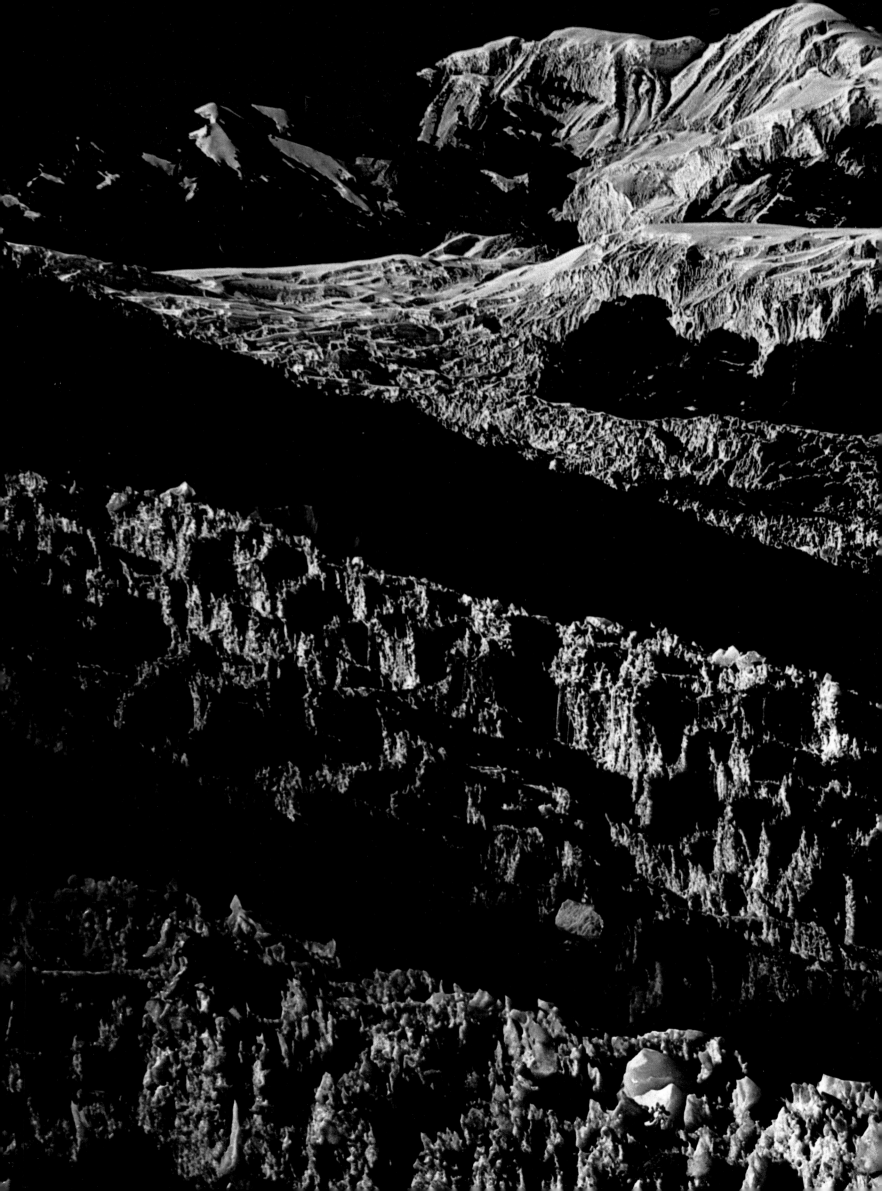

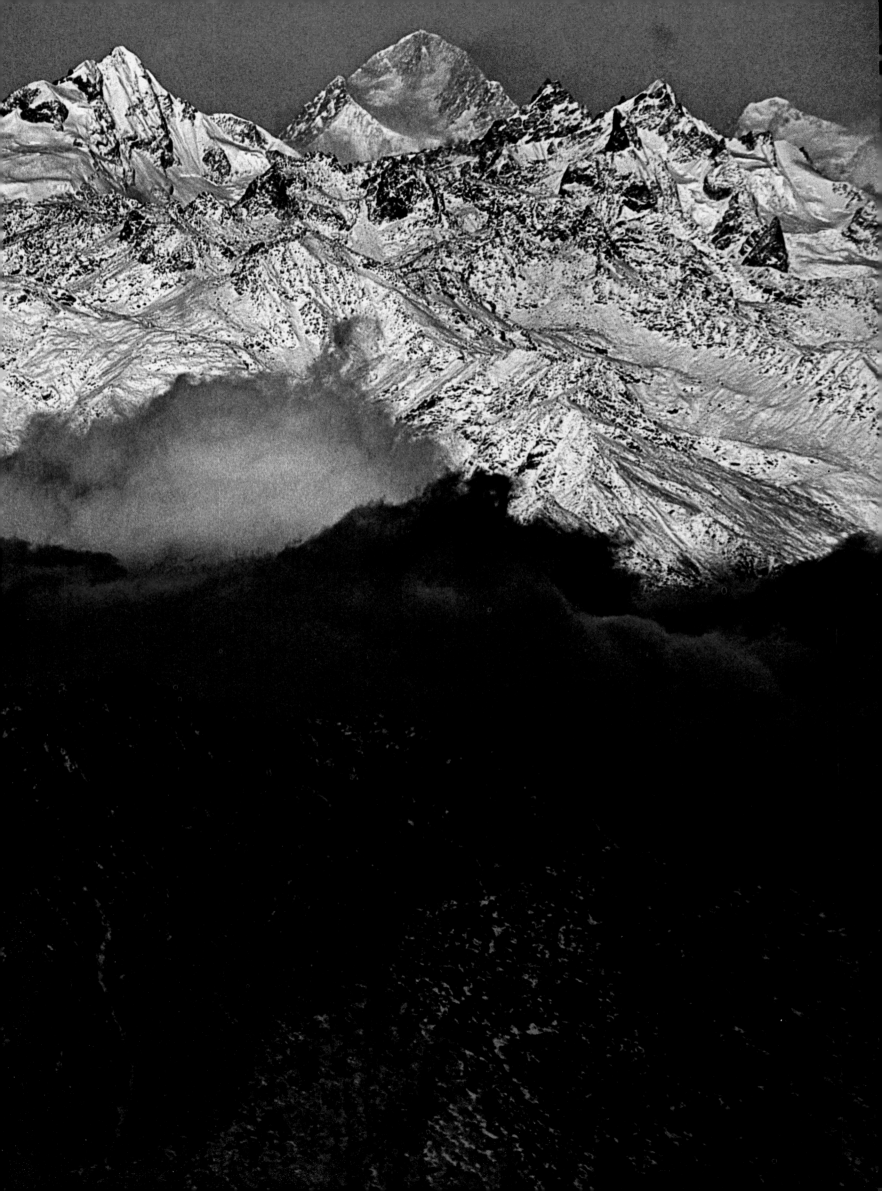

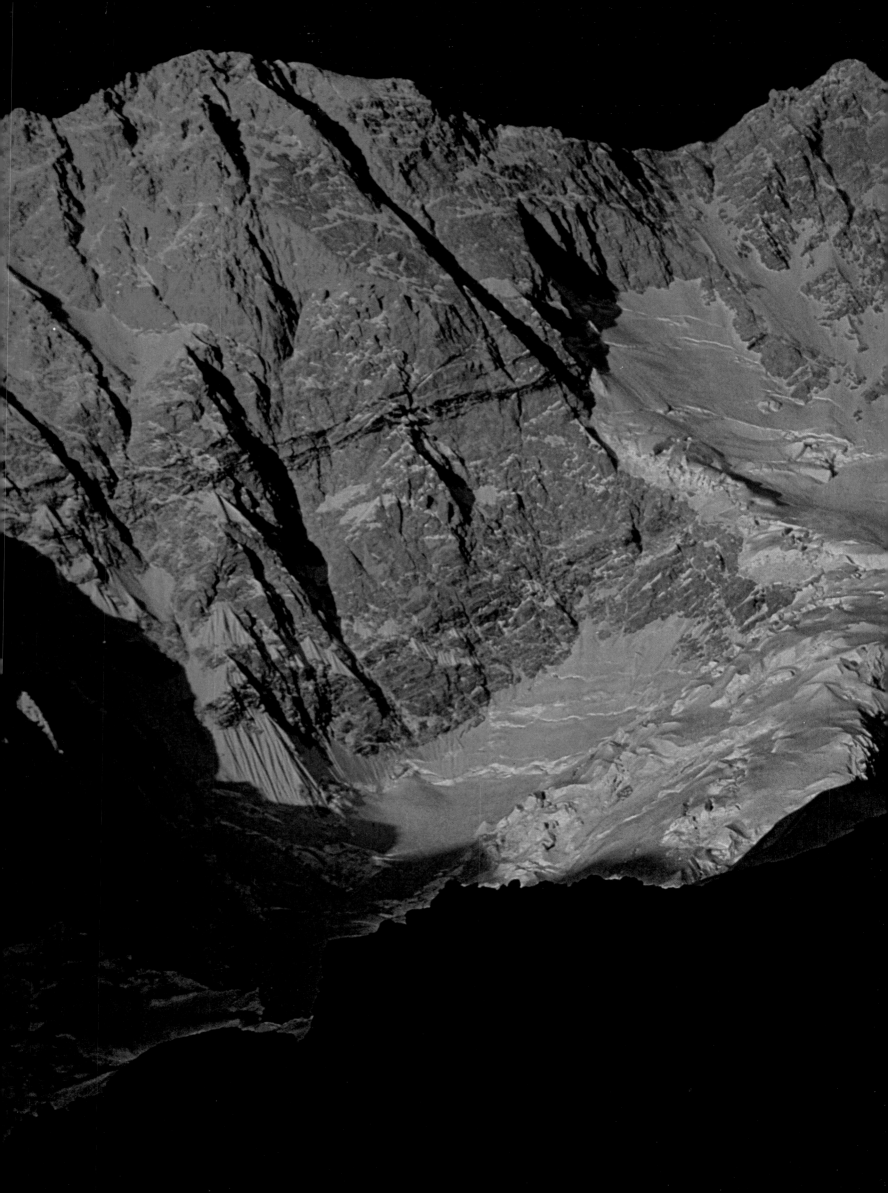

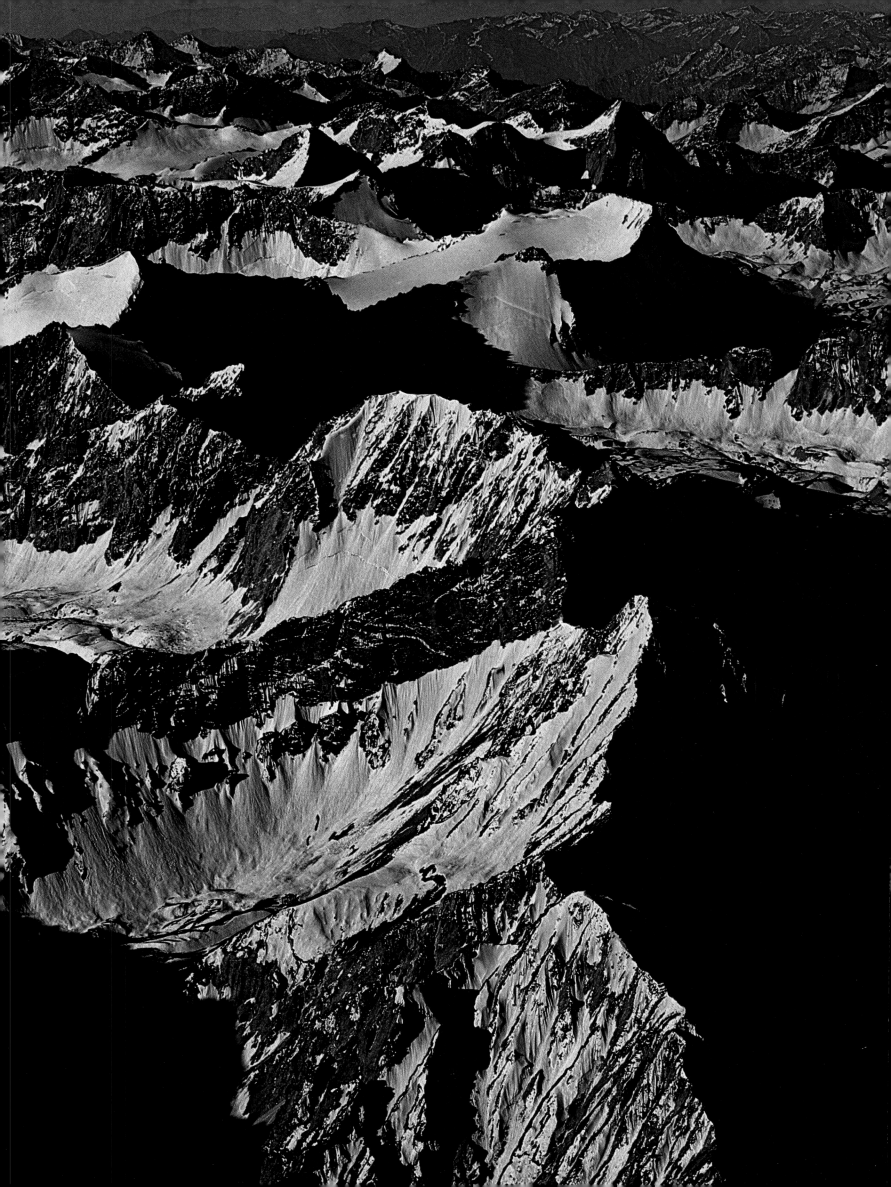

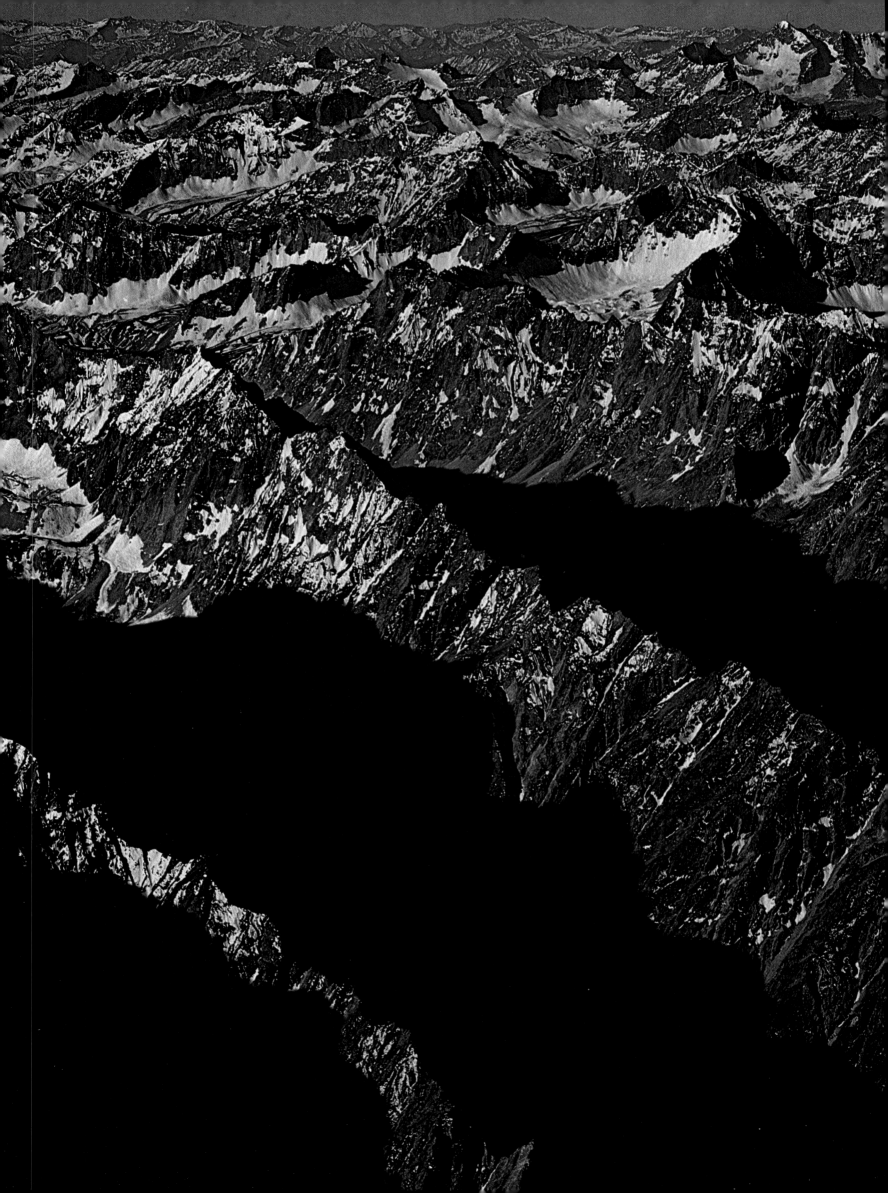

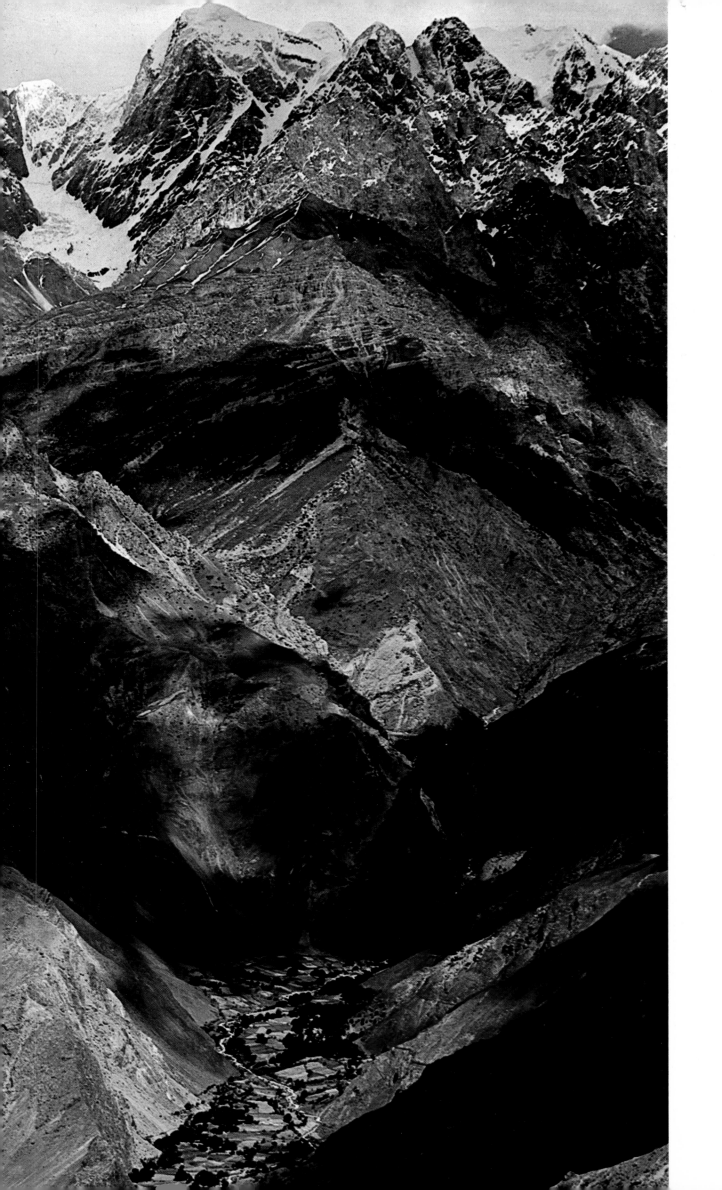

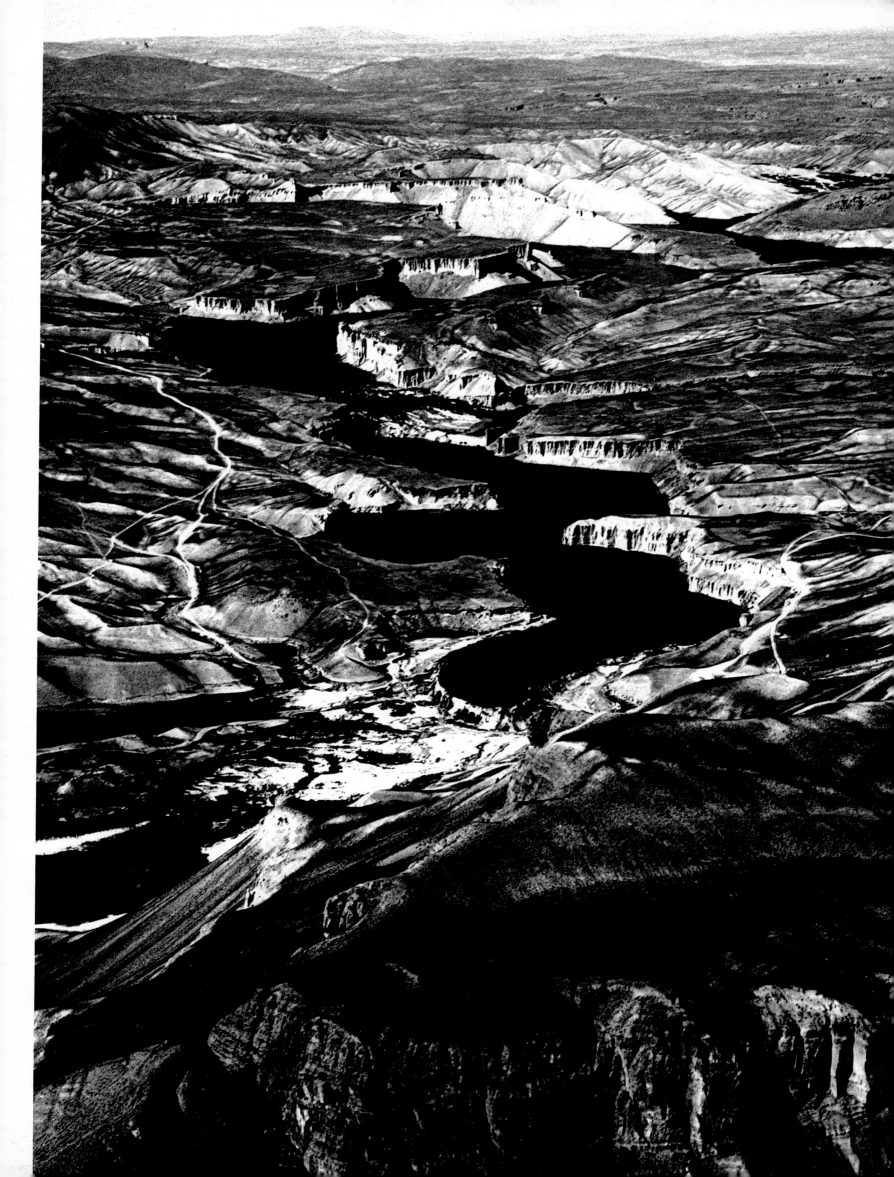

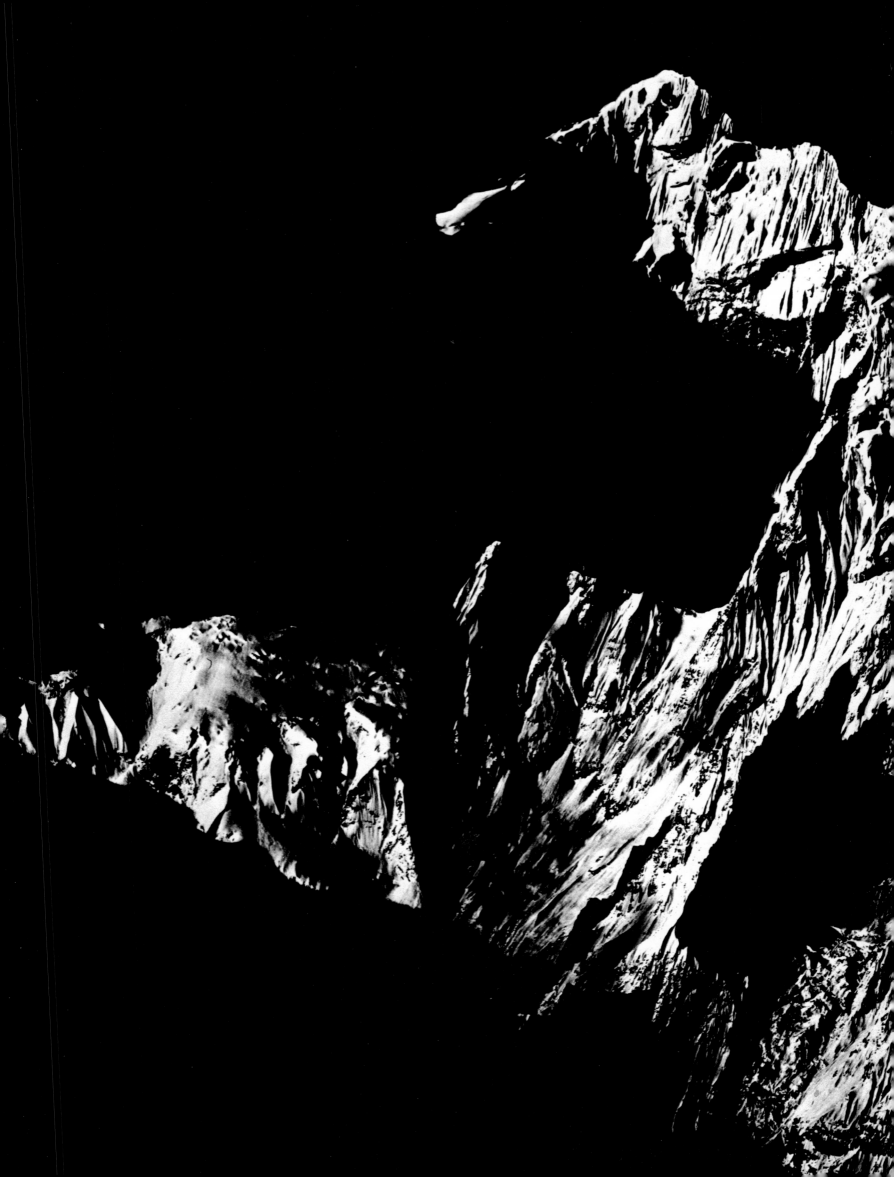

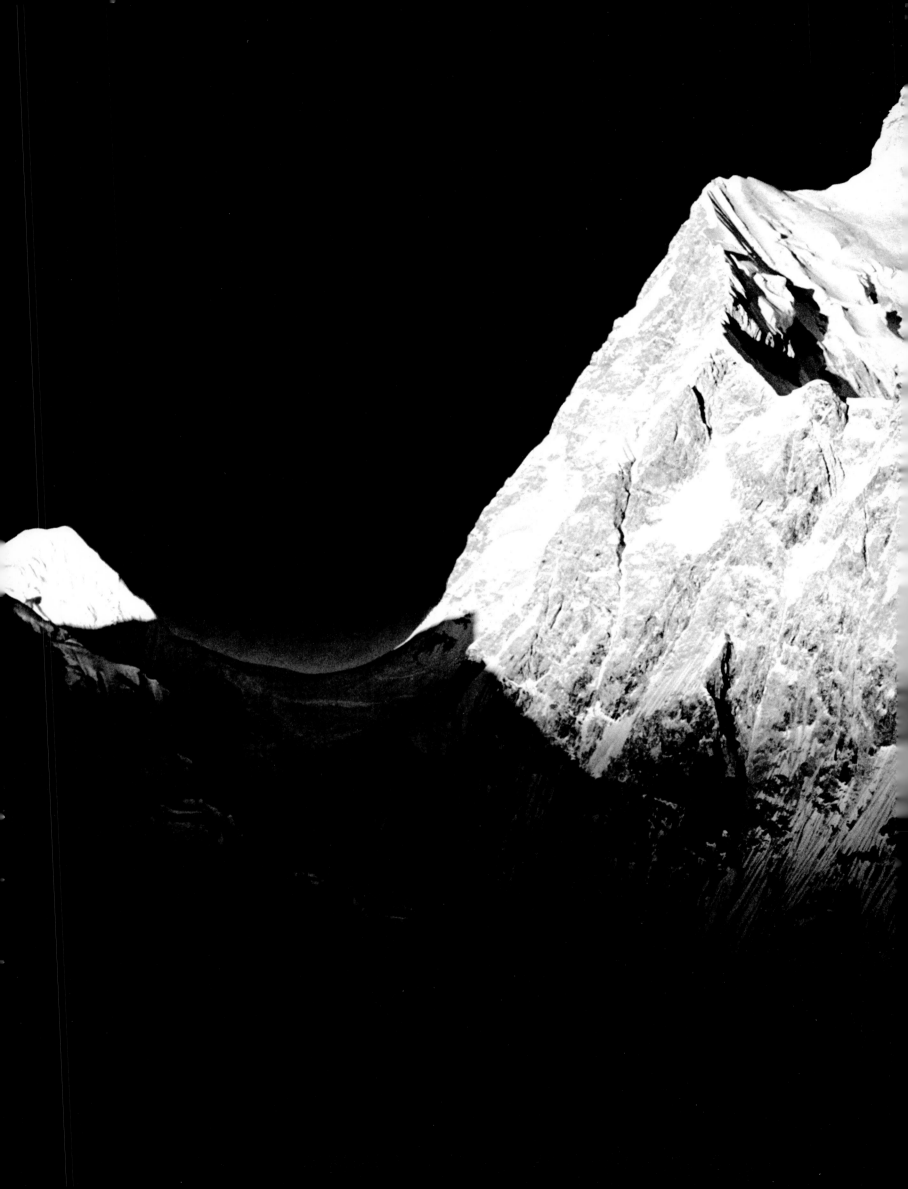

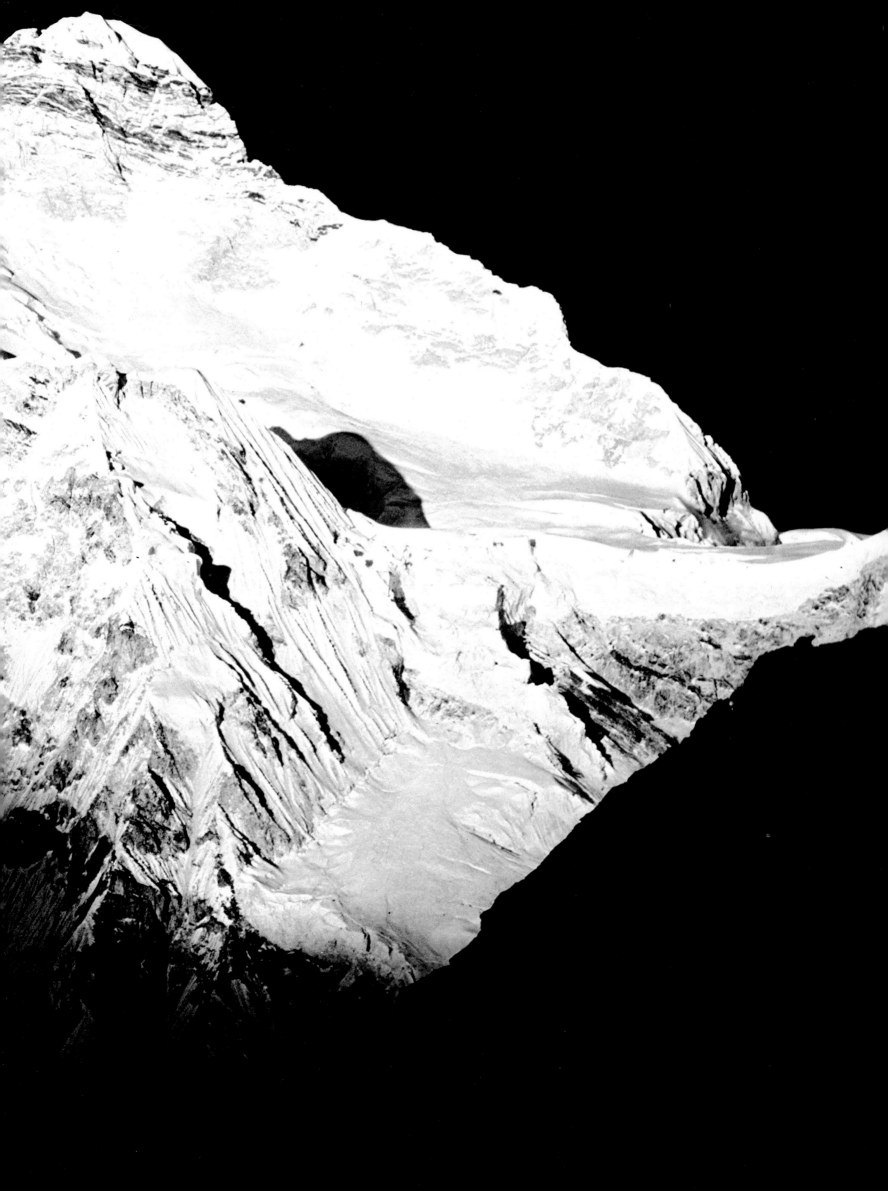

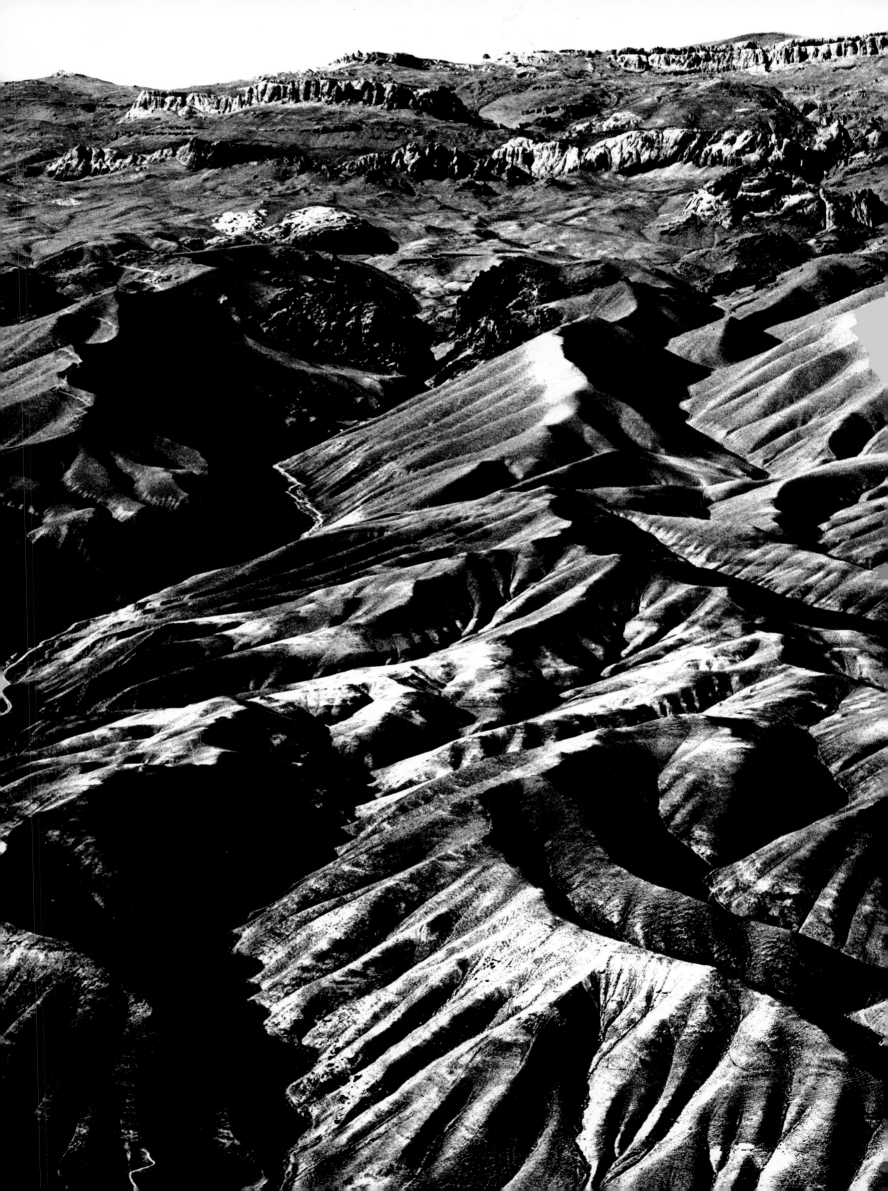

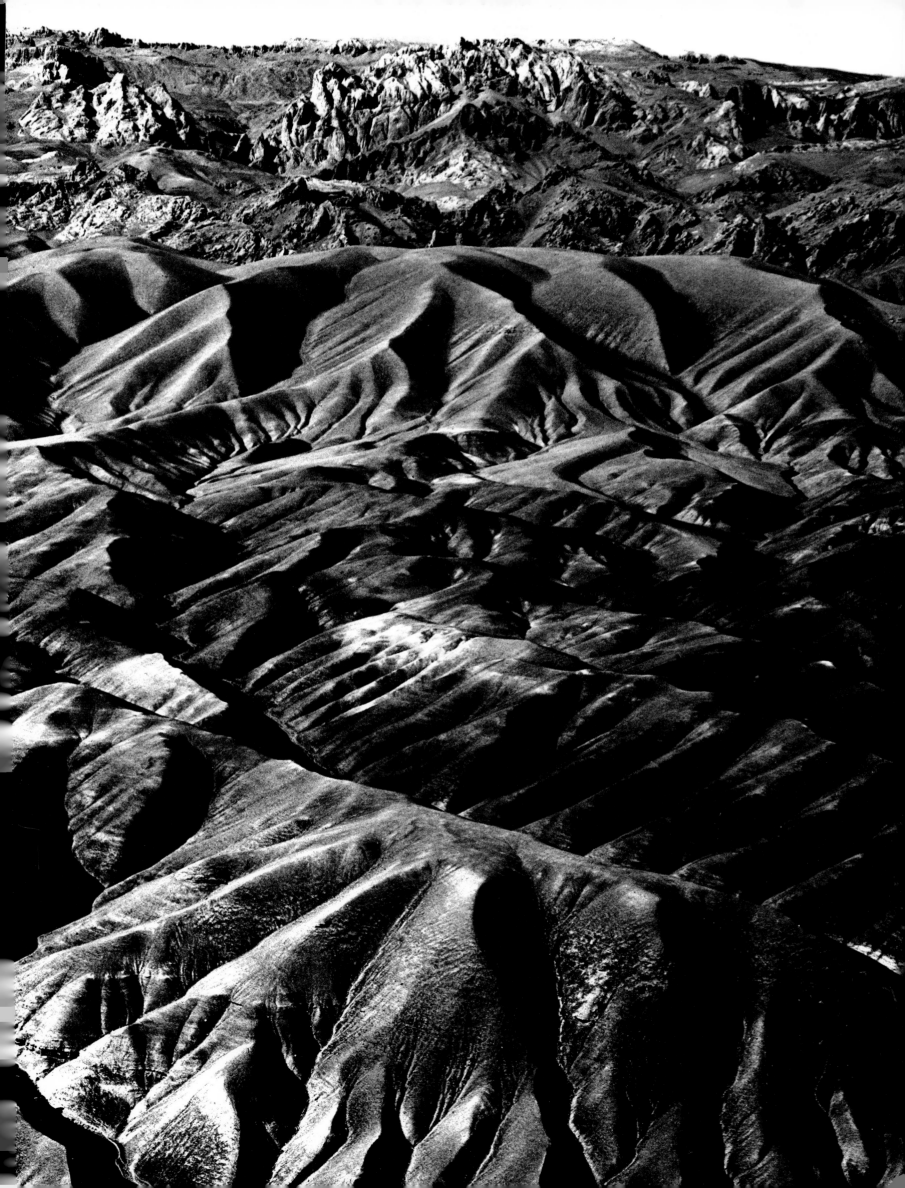

26. JANNU GLACIER

The glacier is viewed from a mountain near Kangbachen Village. The Ghunsa River, which originates from Kangchenjunga Glacier, flows from left to right of the cairn in the foreground; its flow is halted by Jannu Glacier cutting into it from due east. These glaciers have spent themselves, and are in their dying stages.

27. JANNU FROM CHUNJERMA PASS

In 1899 the Italian photographer Vittorio Sella took this same view of Jannu. His was made in September, mine in February. Our camp was pitched in the pass, and my sherpas will not soon forgive me for the ice and the fierce winds we met there. The photograph shows the southwest side of Jannu in late afternoon. In 1962 the French expedition climbed along the ridge seen at the right.

28. SHARPHU

In 1962 Sharphu was discovered when a joint party from two Japanese universities climbed Nupchu. The area has never been surveyed; Sharphu's height, listed on maps as 7,200 meters, is probably an estimate. This photograph was taken from a village in Kangbachen after the tail winds of a blizzard had cleared the skies.

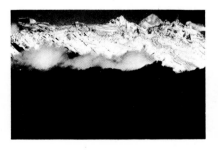

29. UNNAMED PEAK NEAR YALUNG GLACIER

On the left bank of Yalung Glacier this peak was photographed from the moraine at the upper part of the glacier. The foreground rocks appear larger than they are; we climbed up the glacier by jumping from one rock to the next. The surface snow, coated with thin ice, did not hold our weight and we sank deep at every step. Yalung Glacier is quite old, and has shrunk considerably. The drop from moraine to glacier was 100 meters.

30. TELEPHOTO VIEW OF MAKALU

A close-up of the earth's fifth highest peak, Makalu (8,475 meters), taken from Chunjerma Pass. At the left Chamlang (7,319 meters) is partially visible. Everest is on the right. I caught the moment when the light from the rising sun turns its brightest yellow; the yellow will turn slowly whiter, and by 10 A.M. the tone is blue. Clouds start to form after the sun is up. Before I realized it, huge cauliflower-shaped clouds were moving straight toward me.

31. NUPCHU

The route from Kangbachen winds through a valley and up to a wide field called Mindhu, where animals are probably brought to graze in summer; in winter there is no man or animal to be found. Further along this route occurs this view of Nupchu Glacier and Nupchu Icefall; from here the approach to the mountain is fairly easy. An expedition from two Japanese universities first climbed this 7,028-meter mountain in 1962.

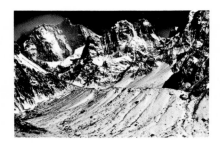

32. JANNU'S NORTH WALL
I took this photograph from a mountain top behind Kangbachen. Jannu is regarded as a fearful mountain, and it can look like a monstrous bird with wings spread. I studied the north face from various angles and became convinced that few rock walls in the Himalayas are so awesome. After examining the summit area with my 500-mm telescopic lens, I believe climbing the wall would be a hopeless task.

33. MOONLIGHT ON JANNU
Light problems make difficult a clear daytime photograph of Jannu's entire north wall. I decided to try it by moonlight, but the phase of the moon was not then ideal and I got this rather flat view. The snow-covered landscape looked blue to the naked eye. The earth's rotation makes stars appear as curved white lines; it was suggested that the bright streak in the photograph might be an orbiting satellite.

34. WEDGE PEAK AT SUNSET
Wedge Peak, 6,750 meters high, viewed from Pang Pema at sundown. The wind blowing across Kangchenjunga Glacier in the evening reverberates against this rock wall with a low, rumbling noise. The Kangchenjunga mountains viewed from Pang Pema are incomparable; we were not authorized to go further north. Ten kilometers beyond is Johnsan Pass, the gateway to Tibet.

35. SIKKIM HIMALAYAS FROM DARJEELING
The Himalaya mountains closest to human habitation are the Sikkims; Darjeeling is 70 kilometers to the south. Tiger Hill, outside Darjeeling, is one of the five best spots for Himalayan photography; its view equals those from Damang Pass and Nagarkot in Nepal. From left to right: Jannu, 7,710 meters; Ratang, 6,678 meters; Kabru, 7,338 meters; Talund, 7,349 meters. Kangchenjunga, 8,598 meters, is in the clouds. At far right is Pandim, 6,691 meters.

36. WEDGE PEAK
This shot is from the large grassy field at Lhonak. From this angle Wedge Peak (6,750 meters) does not look its usual self. The Ghunsa bring animals to the area for pasture in summer, and the stone walls in the foreground form a simple animal pen. The Tibetans believe that the flags in the center will drive away evil spirits; prayers are inscribed on these red and white bits of cloth.

37. SUB-MOUNTAIN OF WEDGE PEAK
This too was photographed from the field at Lhonak. The enclosure in the foreground is an animal shelter. Across from here Kangchenjunga Glacier flows from left to right, and every evening dense fog arises from the lower part of the glacier. Here the sub-mountain of Wedge Peak reflects the evening glow. Tibet is only 15 kilometers to the north.

38. MOUNTAINS AROUND YAMATARI GLACIER
After leaving Chunjerma Pass we camped in a field through which flowed the Mudhimbuk River, actually a stream. Though famed as a campsite, it was covered with snow and not particularly pleasant. Within half a day's climb there is a ridge with a panoramic view of Yamatari Glacier. Jannu lies beyond the left edge of this photograph. What I thought was a mountain here may be only an elevation along a ridge.

39. KANGCHENJUNGA
After a long detour west on the second day of our trip from Tseram along Yalung Glacier, I set up my camera at sunset to photograph the world's third highest mountain. Kangchenjunga's main peak, 8,598 meters, is in the center; to the left is the west peak, and on the right is the south peak, 8,474 meters. The mountain's wall seemed to spew forth red-colored clouds. It was a strange dreamlike scene.

40. TIRICH MIR, EAST FACE
From the middle of Lower Tirich Glacier I caught the moon lingering above the east face of the mountain after sunrise. On the right the east peak, 7,691 meters high, obscures the slightly higher main peak. I worked hard to find the best position; closer to the mountains the peaks looked deceptively low. By moving to the left I could include part of the east peak, but Peak 33 was then hidden behind other mountains; the vantage point here proved the ideal one.

122

41. MID HINDU KUSH

It is hard to believe the earth can look like this, the center of the Afghanistan side of the Hindu Kush mountains. The Koh-i-Yezmi peaks, 5,252 meters, frame the left foreground; the shadowed peak at left above them is 5,315 meters; the white mountain at upper left is 5,457 meters. At the top are the mountains of Koh-i-Sarband-Sagau and a 5,556-meter unnamed peak. At upper right is Koh-i-Kosokar-Gantiwa and its sub-mountains. The Pawloghar River lies shadowed in the right foreground.

42. BUNI ZOM AND ITS SUB-MOUNTAINS

The village in the foreground valley is Reshun. From left to right: Shah Dok, 5,538 meters; the north peak of Buni Zom, 6,338 meters; the main peak, 6,551 meters; the south peak, 6,220 meters (right background). Looming in the center is Khorabohrt Zom, 5,850 meters; the larger white mountain on the right is Chakhori Zom II, 5,957 meters; to its right further back is the main peak, 6,000 meters. All are dry and brown, typical of the Hindu Kush range.

43. BAND-I-AMIR

My climbing friends think that all "real" mountains are covered with snow, and I balk at calling this desert area northwest of Kabul part of the Hindu Kush. But cultural geographers call Bamiyan and Band-i-Amir a basin in the Hindu Kush, so I include the area in this volume. The photograph simply shows a desert lake, but the color of the deep water is beautiful.

44. WOMAN FROM KABUL

Muslim women rarely show their faces, and to be photographed is out of the question. In 1959 western clothing became legal for women, yet many still cling to old customs. A photographer was recently clubbed to death by local residents for trying to photograph a Muslim woman. The residents would have protested to us even if this woman had agreed to pose; for this picture we were rewarded only with rocks and spittle.

45. BAND-I-AMIR AND DESERT

From above, these lakes appear to be at the same altitude; actually they are on a terraced slope. There are also a few waterfalls. In the east there are snow-covered mountains (not visible here). Pilots flying international routes at 8,000 meters are guided by these lakes.

46. WALL ON RIGHT BANK OF RAMTANG GLACIER

To reach the source of this glacier one must walk up the moraine, then on up the glacier. The climb is quite dangerous; rocks fly down from the steep moraine wall. On the right is the frozen north wall of White Wave (6,960 meters). I photographed this part of the wall early in the morning. The ice blocks on the glacier looked like little monsters waking up to dance a welcome to us.

47. JANNU

Jannu is variously called the "Treacherous Mountain," "Sphinx," and "Sleeping Lion," names probably traceable to photographs by the famous Vittorio Sella. I stood at the same place in Chunjerma Pass where he did in 1899. The lapse of time has brought no changes to the shape of the mountain or the sky above it. I was greatly moved as I closed the shutter of my camera.

48. BARREN MOUNTAINS

Steppe and desert meet in this area, 80 kilometers north of Kabul. It does not rain here in summer, and melted snow provides the only water. I have seen the struggle to survive in the cold at Namche Bazar in Nepal, 4,000 meters high; living in this desert can be no less difficult in its way. Small mud cottages are visible here.

49. MOUNTAIN RANGE IN MID HINDU KUSH

In few places are there so many mountains in one area as here. Nepal has countless mountains over 6,000 meters, but they can be sorted into ranges. In the Hindu Kush there are no specially prominent peaks and the mountains are tightly grouped. The one visible in the upper right corner is Koh-i-Mondi, 6,248 meters.

Afterword *Yoshikazu Shirakawa*

I have explored the South Pacific area, and the memory of its great expanses of ocean made the massive icy mountains of the Himalayas even more impressive. My earlier trips to the Alps also motivated me to produce this book; I had visited part of the Himalayas before I went to the Alps, and something kept whispering to me to return to the Himalayas. I left to my publisher the editing of *The Alps* and flew to Kathmandu.

It is difficult to realize that the area of this forbidding mountain chain is rapidly growing in population. Year round the mountain surfaces are plated with a thick layer of ice and many parts of the region are as yet uncharted, although the Himalayan mountains over 8,000 meters have all been scaled.

Bounded by Bhutan in the east and Afghanistan in the west, the Himalayas cover parts of eight countries. Fourteen mountains in the vast 3,000-kilometer expanse are over 8,000 meters high; hundreds are over 7,000 meters; peaks over 6,000 meters are too numerous to count. Everybody knows something about the Himalayas—that they were once under a sea or lake; or that they were formed at approximately the same time as the Alps and the Andes. Beyond this most people have little knowledge about them. Few can visualize the density of these mountains, or have any understanding of the everyday life of the inhabitants.

I decided to travel on foot over as much of the Himalayas as possible and to recount my findings as thoroughly as I could. An exhaustive study would be a superhuman task for one man, but my book would fill some gaps in our knowledge of the region. Marco Polo's reports of his travels first awakened 13th-century European minds to the wonders of Central Asia and the Far East. Six hundred years before him the Chinese priest Hsüan-tsang journeyed across Middle Asia, and British and French translations are now available of his *Record of Western Lands of the Great T'ang Period.* In 1848 Sir Joseph Hooker's *Diary of the Himalayas* described an expedition into the Sikkim Himalayas; the Schlagintweit brothers introduced the world to the Garhwal Himalayas; the British alpinist Gleam explored a number of ranges in the chain, including the Sikkim and Garhwal Himalayas. But the British mountain explorer Douglas W. Freshfield and the world-famous Italian photographer Vittorio Sella made probably the most important journey, circling an extremely wide area including Baltoro Glacier and Kangchenjunga. Freshfield's *Round Kangchenjunga* was written in 1903, and their book of photographs, *The Baltoro Glacier,* introduced the Himalayas to the world.

Nepal, by the Swiss explorer Toni Hagen, investigates the nature and people of that region. He has contributed a wealth of information and is considered a leading authority on the Himalayas, yet he knew only Nepal.

Not long ago a Japanese Alpine photographer published an album entitled *The Himalayas,* a handy volume that helped give an image of the Himalayas to the Japanese; it features a small area of Nepal, just one of the eight countries over which the Himalayan Range lies. *Peaks in the Himalayas,* by Kyuya Fukada, includes a collection of photographs taken by different photographers, the first Japanese book to convey the scope of the Himalayas, but the varying images make a true picture of the mountains hard to discern. I firmly believe that one photographer must be employed to document clearly the many features of the Himalayas.

The Himalayas cover so great an expanse that the weather in the eastern area greatly differs from that farthest west. The eastern end has dry and rainy seasons; in the west the weather is dry the year round and mountains and desert are in stark contrast. Plant and animal life along the range also contrast sharply; the lush green of Nepal bears little resemblance to the barren mountains of Pakistan. Even within Nepal the mountains differ; Everest and its environs do not prepare one for the Annapurna area. One reason why I wanted to compile this book was to see and record as much as I could of the entire region—its similarities and differences.

The Himalayas are both beautiful and perilous, and I wanted to capture this essence. Since few will visit this remote

125

area, I hoped to bring the Himalayas to you. If I have imparted a deeper knowledge of them, I have fulfilled my purpose. I hope that people of the world will better understand the planet on which they live, and consider how their species may best survive. I have reported on 130 countries as fully as possible in the series "World Civilizations and World Geography," "World Civilizations," and others, with the purpose of impressing upon others the need to re-examine the conditions of our world. The vastness of the globe must limit one individual's perspective, but the comments of astronauts, observing the earth from space, have interested me: one deplored it that the earth, covered with green and having abundant air and water, is being polluted; an Apollo 8 astronaut observed that the earth is like an oasis in the treacherous space of the universe; one of Apollo 11's crew said that when he thinks of the universe God created he wonders what man is; Commander Alan Shepard, aboard Apollo 14, said while returning from the moon that it saddened him to look at the earth and think that men were still fighting there.

Human intelligence enabled man to reach the moon, the same intelligence that invented nuclear weapons. Technology has developed a high level of industry and also the complex that is polluting and disrupting nature: pollution is now a common hazard in major cities everywhere. Professor Arnold Toynbee wrote to me: "In photographing the beautiful places of the world, you are doing a great service. Your photographs will have preserved a record of what unspoiled Nature was like, if Man carries his present defacement of Nature to its miserable conclusion. But I hope your photographs will help to deter mankind from continuing on this disastrous course. This would be a great reward for your work." His words encouraged me to continue working on this photographic series, begun over ten years ago.

Space travel is no longer a dream; the medical sciences have made great contributions to mankind; technology advances at a tremendous pace. Yet we have domestic unrest, nations that constantly wage war, and an environment we are ruining every day, bit by bit. My only fear about my work is that I might inadvertently add a single stroke to the blueprint of a plan to desolate the earth.

PHOTOGRAPHING THE HIMALAYAS

The main difficulties in mountain photography are strong natural light and severe climatic conditions. Cameras must have simple mechanisms, reliable enough to operate under the worst conditions. Equipment must be lightweight, particularly where transportation facilities are poor and heights of 6,000 to 7,000 meters are common. With these considerations in mind I chose the following equipment:

Cameras:		Asahi Pentax (6x7) 3
		Asahi Pentax (SP) 3
Lenses:	(1)	for Asahi Pentax (6x7)
		Super Takumar 55mm f/3.5
		Super Takumar 75mm f/4.5
		Super Takumar 105mm f/2.4
		Super Takumar 200mm f/4
		Super Takumar 300mm f/4
	(2)	for Asahi Pentax (SP)
		Super Takumar 55mm f/1.8
		Super Takumar 28mm f/3.5
		Super Takumar 135mm f/3.5

Since replacements could not be obtained in the Himalayas, I carried three cameras and two lenses of each size. I kept camera-lens combinations as simple as possible: oxygen is extremely thin at 7,000 meters and one's normal functions slow down considerably. I wanted to be able to change lenses and operate my camera almost without thinking, even at high altitudes: the camera's operation must be simple and the photographer completely familiar with his equipment, to work under any conditions. With these precautions I successfully completed my photographic expedition despite the high altitudes in the Everest region—and attacks of mountain sickness.

To protect my cameras and accessory equipment during transport I wrapped everything in numerous vinyl coverings. My main concern was sand. It almost never rains in eastern Nepal and constant winds blow a fine sand that could ruin all photographs if it got inside the cameras. Pakistan and Afghanistan have desert regions and present the same problem of sand. Protection against cold was also a concern: a camera mechanism must operate at temperatures of $-20°$ to $-40°C$. I had my cameras and lenses winterized before leaving Japan, but took care to insert new batteries every five days. At normal temperatures batteries are good for 10,000 shutter closings, but their efficiency drops 50 per cent at $0°$ C. I kept the used batteries, for they regain effectiveness in normal temperatures.

Throughout my expedition I avoided tricky exposure techniques. Lens apertures ranged from f/16 to f/45, depending on conditions. The Asahi Pentax's "Spotmeter" accurately selected the exposure time, usually 1/30 second to one second. I exposed for 1–3 minutes when photographing the mountains in moonlight. Although a fish-eye lens provides interesting